CROWNED WITH GLORY & HONOR

What are human beings
that you are mindful of them,
mortals that you care for them?
Yet you have made them a little lower than God,
and crowned them with glory and honor.
—Psalm 8:4-5

But we do see Jesus,
who for a little while was made lower than the angels,
now crowned with glory and honor because of the suffering of
death, so that by the grace of God he might taste death for everyone.
—Hebrews 2:9

Studies in Peace and Scripture Series

Volumes in the Studies in Peace and Scripture Series are sponsored by the Institute of Mennonite Studies, Elkhart, Indiana, and released by a variety of publishers.

CROWNED WITH GLORY & HONOR

Human Rights in the Biblical Tradition

Christopher D. Marshall

Foreword by Glen Stassen

Studies in Peace and Scripture, Volume 6

Pandora Press U.S.
Telford, Pennsylvania

copublished with
Herald Press
Scottdale, Pennsylvania and

Lime Grove House
Auckland, New Zealand

Pandora Press U.S. orders, information, reprint permissions:
pandoraus@netreach.net
1-215-723-9125
126 Klingerman Road, Telford PA 18969
www.PandoraPressUS.com
To purchase in New Zealand, Australia, Singapore, and Malaysia, contact
Lime Grove House, our exclusive distributor for those areas, at
64-9-585-0023 (phone/fax), PO Box 37-955, Parnell, Auckland NZ;
61-2-9871-3137 (phone), 61-2-9871-2869 (fax), PO Box 1704 Rozelle, NSW,
Sydney, Australia; or limegrovehouse@hotmail.com

Library of Congress Cataloguing-in-Publication Data
Marshall, Christopher D.
  Crowned with glory and honor: human rights in the biblical
tradition / Christopher D. Marshall ; foreword by Glen Stassen
    p. cm. -- (Studies in peace and scripture series; v. 6)
  Includes bibliographical references and index.
  ISBN 1-931038-04-X (trade paper : alk. paper)
    1. Human rights--Biblical teaching. 2. Human rights--Religious
aspects--Christianity.
  I. Title. II. Studies in peace and scripture ; v. 6

BS680.H85 M37 2002
261.7--dc21
                                                    2001044792

10 09 08 07 06 05 04 03 02   10 9 8 7 6 5 4 3 2 1

For
Willard Swartley,
colleague, friend, guide, and inspiration

ἡγεῖσθαι αὐτοὺς
ὑπερεκπερισσοῦ ἐυ ἀγάπη δὰ
τὸ ἔργου αὐτῶυ
—1 Thessalonians 5:13

Contents

Foreword

CHRISTOPHER MARSHALL HAS WRITTEN A WONDERFUL book. It will be enormously helpful to Christians who love "the least of these" (Matt 25:45), those millions of people created in the image of God and loved by God but who are being victimized by forces of injustice or evil, the powers and authorities, or merely those satisfied with their current privileges. Focus on human rights draws our attention to any whose human dignity, created in God's image, is being violated.

Marshall is a New Testament scholar with rare ethical perceptiveness, not only in this book but in his others. He provides a drama-and-narrative approach to biblical theology and ethics as grounding for human rights. His use of Richard Hays' paradigmatic approach to biblical ethics is especially helpful for avoiding both legalism and vague abstraction. His biblical paradigms of creation, stewardship, covenant, incarnation, church, and eschatological consummation provide a richer understanding of human rights than other approaches. His biblical perspective corrects an Enlightenment approach to human rights that overemphasizes individualistic liberty.

Marshall insists that rights to life, equality, and participation are as important as rights to freedom. This emphasis is especially needed for readers in the United States. One could add what is surely biblical: rights of *membership in community*, and rights of communities themselves to be sustained.[1]

In support of Marshall, let me tell a story I learned from my former teacher, Heinz Eduard Tödt of the University of Heidelberg.[2] When the concept of human rights first developed during the 1645 movement for religious liberty among free church Puritans in England, German culture was influenced by France. Thus German churches learned about human rights not from Christians in England but mistakenly thought such rights originated in the later anti-church and even atheistic French Enlightenment. So they opposed human rights.

This fit conservative tendencies that wed church and state, "Throne and Altar," wanting the church (Altar) to support the German Emperor (Throne). Hence when Germany finally experimented with democracy during the Weimar Republic (1919-1932), churches mostly yearned for a return to monarchy and opposed democracy. This contributed to the defeat of Weimar democracy and the victory of the authoritarian Nazi Party and Adolf Hitler as *der Führer.*

Then as Hitler implemented his massacre of six million Jews, Poles, homosexuals, and Marxists in the Holocaust, the Germans lacked the commitments to human rights that might have enabled them to oppose such evil. Most stood by or even supported what Hitler was doing.[3] The erroneous understanding of the origin of human rights, and the Germans' authoritarian opposition to human rights, led the churches into shocking error. As a result millions of innocent victims died and the witness of the churches was greatly weakened. Germany is now extensively secular. After World War II and German repentance for the evils of Naziism, Germans realized the error of their dismissal of human rights. Ernst Troeltsch and Georg Jellinek pointed out that human rights had originated among free church Puritans in England, not a half-century later in the Enlightenment. German Christians now understand they need a plumbline of justice to guard against injustice perpetrated by the powerful.

In reaction to the evils of the Nazi period, and in response to the need of colonies for independence from colonial masters, a worldwide movement for human rights has arisen. Shortly after World War II, The United Nations Declaration of Human Rights was written, then signed by the majority of nations. Most major church groups support human rights, as do most Christian ethicists. As Marshall writes, "Human rights have become an almost universal currency of moral debate."

If Christians are to debate over justice for those being violated, we have to learn the language. But we also have to bring a biblical corrective of Enlightenment individualism.

The German authoritarian error is a cautionary tale for all of us. We still hear echoes of that old authoritarian resistance to human rights, and claims that such rights are Enlightenment property. During the U.S. civil rights struggle, segregationists argued Christians should not advocate human rights but be willing to give up their rights. During the struggle for freedom in Eastern Europe against Communist dictatorship, dictatorial governments made it illegal to speak of human rights. During the struggle of women for basic equality, some said women should submit to authority. They failed to say what the apostle Paul did—that servanthood should be mutual and both husband and wife should affirm each other's rights (Eph 5:21 and 1 Cor 7:3-5). Opposition to rights has functioned historically, if unintentionally, to maintain privileges of the privileged and undercut the struggle for justice of the violated. Support for human rights has spread democracy.

Christians rightly say we should outdo each other in showing love and honor to others rather than focusing only on what is right for ourselves (Rom. 12:9-10). From the perspective of the privileged, human rights often look like the self-assertion of those whose rights they resist. From the perspective of the deprived, human rights usually look like the essential requirements of justice. From the perspective of Christians who know God cares especially for the weak and the violated, human rights focus attention on those most likely to be deprived of their rights: widows and orphans who lack a man in a patriarchal society, the poor who lack money in a materialistic society, the outsiders and outcasts who lack belonging in an in-group society. As Marshall writes, the majority affirm human rights because of their usefulness in the struggle against oppression and injustice. A right is a duty of others to defend those whose legitimate rights are denied.

I want to add support to Marshall's mention of the three historical origins of human rights (p. 32), and to Tödt's historical narrative. In 1645 Richard Overton originated the concept of human rights. Overton had been a member of the first Baptist church in history, the congregation of John Smyth that emigrated to Holland in search of religious liberty and joined with the Waterlander Mennonite Congregation. Eventually Overton returned to England and a Baptist church there. His concept of human rights began with booklets he published arguing against religious persecution and for religious liberty.

Thrown in jail for his writings, he argued for the right of freedom of the press. In jail, he got to know the poor who had been jailed for their debts. They were not even fed. Conditions were horrible. Sensitized to their basic needs, he argued for the rights of housing and care for poor orphans and widows, the aged and the handicapped, and the right to education and land. The result was a remarkably comprehensive doctrine of human rights, including freedoms of religious and civil liberty and equal treatment before the law; basic needs and economic rights; and rights of participation in choosing the government and in urging just policies by the government.

Like a human baby, human rights was born with all its dimensions already present in 1645, from the pen of an Anabaptist/Baptist, a half-century before the Enlightenment. Overton argued based on paradigms analogous to those Marshall develops: the Lordship of Christ over ecclesiastical hierarchy and over human consciences; "the peace of our Sovereign Lord and King" over against wars of religion; the great commission (Matt. 28:19 ff.) to teach discipleship, not force it; biblical justice for the poor "who have not bread to still the cry of their children"; creation of all in the image of God; separation of church and state and biblical teachings on the limits of governmental authority; Christ's teaching that we are not to lord it over one another as the Gentiles do; and the Golden Rule.

The result is a rich triad of rights much like those Marshall develops, not only an assertion of individual liberties. Human rights did not first emerge later in the Enlightenment, and rights in recent times have come not from the Enlightenment but from the struggle of underdogs against authoritarians. Let us not repeat the error of Weimar Germany's rights opponents[4] but learn from Marshall's biblical and ethical insights.

—*Glen Stassen, Lewis Smedes Professor of Ethics,*
   Fuller Theological Seminary, Pasadena, California

Series Preface

VISIONS OF PEACE ABOUND IN THE BIBLE, whose pages are also filled with the language and the reality of war. In this respect, the Bible is thoroughly at home in the modern world, whether as a literary classic or as a unique sacred text. This is, perhaps, a part of the Bible's realism: bridging the distance between its world and our own is a history filled with visions of peace accompanying the reality of war. That alone would justify study of peace and war in the Bible. However, for those communities in which the Bible is sacred Scripture, the matter is more urgent. For them, it is crucial to understand what the Bible says about peace—and about war. These issues have often divided Christians from each other, and the way Christians have understood them has had terrible consequences for Jews and, indeed, for the world. A series of scholarly investigations cannot hope to resolve these issues, but it can hope, as this one does, to aid our understanding of them.

The close association of peace and war in the Bible raises serious questions for the contemporary appropriation of Scripture. Are human freedom, justice, and liberation—and the liberation of creation—furthered or hindered by the martial, frequently royal, and pervasively masculine terms in which the Bible speaks of peace? These questions cannot be answered by the rigorous and critical exegesis of the biblical texts alone; they demand serious moral and theological reflection as well. But that reflection will be substantially aided by exegetical studies of the kind included in this series, even as these studies will be illumined by including just that kind of reflection within them.

"Studies in Peace and Scripture" is sponsored by the Institute of Mennonite Studies, the research agency of the Associated Mennonite Biblical Seminary. The seminary and the tradition it represents have a particular interest in peace and, even more so, an abiding interest in the Bible. We hope that this ecumenical series will contribute to a deeper understanding of both.

—*Ben C. Ollenburger, Old Testament Editor, and*
  Willard M. Swartley, New Testament Editor

Author's Preface

THIS BOOK OWES ITS ORIGIN TO AN INVITATION I received to contribute to a symposium in Wellington, New Zealand, in 1998, marking the fiftieth anniversary of the signing of the *Universal Declaration of Human Rights*. I was asked to speak on human rights in the biblical tradition, while others were commissioned to deal with human rights in the theological, legal and political traditions.

I accepted the invitation for mainly selfish reasons. Although a New Testament scholar by training and a longtime member of Amnesty International, I had given comparatively little thought to how my concern for human rights squared with the witness and world view of the Christian Scriptures. The symposium offered an opportunity to explore this connection in more detail.[1]

As I began working on my paper, I soon became aware of just how vast and complex the field of human rights discourse has become over the last fifty years. There are few areas of contemporary life that human rights thinking has not touched. Perhaps most striking is the way human rights categories have become an almost universal currency of moral debate. Rights language is prevalent in the discussion of all kinds of issues, from the personal to the political, from the trivial to the terrifying

One gauge of this is the frequency with which rights terminology figures in newspaper articles on current events. Once I made a point of collecting articles over several weeks from the two newspapers I usually read in which some explicit reference to human rights is made. A brief survey of these articles will show how pervasive and diverse human rights issues are today.

Some of the articles deal with so-called "gross violations" of human rights, such as arbitrary arrest, torture, forced labor, and summary execution. One cites Amnesty International's estimate that daily violations of human rights occur in at least 144 countries in the world. In Tibet, children as young as six have been detained and tortured by Chinese police. So widespread is the practice of torture, according to another report, that over 220 organizations have sprung up around world for treating torture victims and their families. In the United States alone, there are twenty-four torture rehabilitation programs in operation.

One article reports on Amnesty International taking up the case of a seventeen-year-old girl in Nigeria sentenced to 180 lashes for having premarital sex with three men. Other articles deal with human rights abuses during the Bosnian and Kosovo conflicts. One tells of how the International War Crimes Tribunal for Yugoslavia meeting in the Hague has deemed, for the first time in history, the systematic rape of Muslim women to be a crime against humanity, and sentenced some of those responsible for instigating such organized terror to long periods of imprisonment.

Another article reports on a parallel tribunal convened by the Milosovec regime in Belgrade at which charges were laid against fourteen Western leaders for crimes against humanity during the Kosovo bombing campaign. The prosecutor called for maximum jail terms for Bill Clinton and the other NATO leaders, while their Serbian-appointed "defense" lawyer actually demanded their execution!

Another extreme violation of human rights is slavery. According to one report, slavery is more widespread today than at any other time in human history. It is estimated that at its height, the Roman Empire absorbed some 500,000 slaves a year, while over 350 years the trans-Atlantic slave trade transported 13 million people from Africa. Today, a British sociologist estimates, some 27 million people live as slaves, especially debt-slaves. This is at least six times more than 150 years ago.[2]

Human rights language is not confined to accounts of such flagrant and historic injustices as slavery and torture. In some newspaper reports, local criminal violence and its consequences is depicted in rights categories.

In a widely publicized court case in New Zealand, the stepfather of a teenage girl who was abducted by a neighbor, sexually violated, then buried alive was convicted of repeatedly threatening to kill her murderer should he ever be released from prison. Public sympathy for the stepfather was overwhelming. Some politicians hailed him as a hero, and popular demonstrations were staged outside courts throughout the land during his trial. One supporter said of the girl's killer, "People like him should be killed as well. When you commit that kind of crime, you give up your rights. That kind of person is not even human any more."[3]

The stepfather was convicted and received a suspended prison sentence. In agreeing with the judge's decision, one newspaper columnist criticized the public lust for vengeance and insisted that even the likes of the child's murderer "still have basic human rights and a decent society ensures those rights are upheld."[4] A flood of angry letters to the editor ensued criticizing the column's viewpoint.

The link between crime and human rights emerges in another report of a formal complaint lodged with the United Nations Human Rights Commissioner accusing the Australian government of breaching human rights by employing mandatory sentencing laws in the Northern Territory. Such laws, it is argued, remove judicial discretion and breach people's right to a fair hearing. They also indirectly discriminate against the indigenous Aboriginal population who have experienced a sharp increase in imprisonment rates for minor property offences since the laws were introduced.

Several articles deal with issues of sexual and reproductive ethics in terms of rights. One recounts arguments in favor of decriminalizing prostitution in New Zealand, on grounds that present legislation unjustly discriminates against the rights of prostitutes. Another tells of a complaint laid with the New Zealand Human Rights Commission against an Asian airline for refusing to transfer frequent flyer air points to the partners of passengers in de facto or same-sex relationships. In another case brought to the same Commission, a couple with five children won a government payout after being refused permission to have another child using a surrogate mother. The couple claimed they were being discriminated against on grounds of age and family status.

Provisions in New Zealand's human rights legislation for prosecuting people who incite racial disharmony are mentioned in a lengthy article criticizing an Appeal Court decision permitting the distribution of fundamentalist Christian videos attacking homosexuality. The Chief Film Censor had deemed the videos to be hate propaganda and banned their release, a decision upheld by the High Court. However the decision was reversed by the Court of Appeal because it infringed the rights to freedom of speech and belief, as enshrined in the New Zealand Bill of Rights.

A similar clash of rights is reported in another article referring to a Supreme Court ruling in the United States upholding the exclusion of gays from being troop leaders in the Boy Scouts. To force this private organization to observe gay rights, the Supreme Court decided, would violate its right to freedom of association.

In yet another case turning on discrimination, a widower has sued the British government under new human rights legislation for discriminating against him as a man because he is not entitled to receive the same benefits and pensions as a widow is. An article entitled, "Is Part-Time Work a Mum's Right?" deals with discrimination against women in the labor force. The piece describes "a looming human rights battle" in New Zealand over discriminatory behavior against women when they return to work from parental leave.

Discrimination against children features in reports on debates over the rights of children. One conservative columnist dismisses the whole idea of children's rights, as set forth in the United Nations Convention of the Rights of the Child, as "one of the poisonous effects of political correctness on the community."[5] Another article reports that discrimination against minority groups has fueled a campaign by the *Guardian* newspaper in Britain against the legality of the British monarchy. The newspaper's lawyers intend to argue in court that the eighteenth-century legislation barring non-Protestants and those born out of wedlock from succeeding to the British throne is discriminatory, hence illegal under European human rights legislation to which British law must now conform.

Finally, a number of newspaper articles discuss the simmering debate in New Zealand over medically assisted euthanasia, following its legalization in Holland and, for a short time, in one Australian state. Opposition to the law change has come especially from Christian churches, with the Vatican denouncing the Dutch decision as a "violation of human dignity." In an angry rejoinder, one newspaper columnist thunders, "We all have the right to die in dignity; the real violation of human dignity is leaving the terminally ill patient in agony to wait for death."[6]

Even this limited sample of newspaper reports demonstrates how widespread human rights themes have become in contemporary discussion, and how sharply disputed their application to specific issues can be. It would appear, then, that if Christians are to engage meaningfully with the great moral issues of our day, they will need to master the rhetoric of rights and to use it sensitively to articulate key Christian insights and perspectives.

At the same time, Christians will also have to recognize the limits of a rights-based morality. The language of rights is strikingly limited in traditional Christian sources, and a one-sided emphasis on individual rights can obscure the characteristic Christian stress on duty and self-sacrifice.

Yet it is the argument of this book that the notion of human rights is deeply, and uniquely, grounded in the biblical story and that Christians therefore have something special to say about human rights. It is something that *validates* the modern quest to identify and respect human rights; it is something that *enriches* the secular human rights tradition at several key points; and it is something that offers a *corrective* to the growing tendency in contemporary Western society to divorce rights from responsibilities and to conceive of human relationships as a kind of negotiated truce in a battle of competing claims.

So profound is the biblical story's insight into the meaning of being human, so consistent, so uncompromising, is its insistence on human dignity, that those who look to the Christian Scriptures for guidance in this area should become both the world's greatest champions of human rights and the world's greatest critics of rights gone awry. I hope this little book will serve to inform Christian thinking and Christian action in both these respects.

—*Chris Marshall*
  Auckland, New Zealand

CROWNED
WITH GLORY
& HONOR

1
What Are
Human Rights?

THE FIFTIETH ANNIVERSARY OF THE SIGNING of the Universal Declaration of Human Rights (UDHR) was celebrated around the world on December 10, 1998. The adoption of this document without dissent by the General Assembly of the United Nations may rightly be seen as one of the defining moments of modern history. Its thirty brief Articles, which are proclaimed as "a common standard of achievement for all peoples and all nations," set forth rights and freedoms held to be applicable to all human beings "without distinction as to race, color, sex, language, religion, political or other opinion, national or social origin, property, birth or other status."

Although never intended as a legally enforceable treaty, the UDHR, together with its associated Covenants of 1966 and 1976 (known collectively as the "International Bill of Rights"), has acquired a juridical importance far beyond its original intention. It has been widely used by international, regional and even national courts as a point of reference for judging compliance with human rights obligations under the UN Charter. (The full text of the UDHR is included in an Appendix at the end of this book.)

Even more remarkable than the Declaration's impact on international law has been the extent to which human rights language has entered global ethical consciousness. In international relations, human rights serves as a recognized standard of accountability for actions of governments and states.

At the domestic level, too, human rights play a central role in the discussion of all kinds of contentious moral and political issues. Protagonists on both sides of the abortion debate, for example, claim to be champions of human rights, one side asserting the "right to life" of the unborn child, the other side "the right to choose" of the woman. We also hear of the rights of smokers, the rights of prisoners, the rights of patients, the rights of homosexuals to marry and bring up children, the right of the terminally ill to choose when to die, the right of workers to statutory holidays, and the rights of indigenous peoples to customary resources.

Whatever the issue, people at opposite ends of the ideological spectrum agree on at least one thing—that the vocabulary of rights is the best way to stake their ground. Rights has become our favored idiom for articulating fundamental social values and our preferred strategy for clarifying and resolving areas of social conflict.

The strong appeal of rights language is also apparent in contemporary theological discussion. Historically Christian churches have been cautious, if not overtly hostile, to any assertion of "natural rights" or "the rights of man," fearing its non-theistic tone and its potential to weaken the traditional Christian emphasis on obligation. But over the twentieth century, and especially since World War II, most major Christian traditions have issued official statements on human rights. The present vitality of rights language has even affected Bible translation. Whereas commentators once commonly noted that the term *rights* did not even appear in the Bible, much less *human rights*, the New Revised Standard Version uses the term on at least fourteen occasions.[7]

But is this simply an accommodation to modern jargon? Does the ancient biblical text really address itself to human rights? Is it possible to discover a biblical foundation for modern human rights doctrine? Does the Christian faith have anything distinctive to offer the current debate on human rights?[8] Or is the Christian discussion simply a restatement of secular convictions in religious terminology? To what extent is it even valid to seek specific religious foundations for a concept which, by definition, claims for itself a universal validity, transcending all provincial religious perspectives? These are some of the questions to be explored in this book. First, however, more needs to be said about the language and meaning of rights.

SEMANTIC AND CONCEPTUAL PROBLEMS

The term *rights* is employed today in a wide range of legal, moral, philosophical, and political contexts. It has therefore acquired a bewildering diversity of meanings. There are positive rights and negative rights, active rights and passive rights, individual rights and collective rights, moral rights and legal rights, civil rights and political rights, innate rights and natural rights, animal rights and environmental rights, constitutional rights and customary rights, fundamental rights and consequent rights, conjugal rights and reproductive rights, and many more besides.

Some rights are factual descriptions of what "is." Others are normative claims for what "ought" to be. Some are capable of legal enforcement, others are not. Whether rights are best understood as claims, powers, liberties, limits, entitlements, immunities, interests, benefits or a mixture of several categories, is still disputed in philosophical and juridical discussion.[9] Even the key terms used to clarify rights, such as freedom and equality, are dogged with their own ambiguity.[10]

The specific designation *human* rights participates in this semantic confusion. The phrase is sometimes used to describe political or legal provisions; at other times to designate prepolitical or ethical convictions; at still other times it indicates moral or political aspirations. On some occasions it is used as a generic category to embrace all justifiable claims made on behalf of the human race; on other occasions it is used for a limited set of principles against which positive law and moral practice should be measured. Some theorists regard human rights as the minimal requirements for human existence; others treat them as the requisite ingredients for securing communal harmony and social justice.

The epistemological questions surrounding rights are even more involved. Where do rights come from? Are they of divine, natural or human origin? How are they to be known—

by reason, revelation, intuition, demonstrated utility or social consensus? Are they self-evident? If so, why have they only been codified in modern times, and only in the Western tradition? Are rights absolute, universal, and inalienable? Or are they relative to particular cultures and revocable in certain circumstances? Are all rights of equal importance or do they form a hierarchy, either intrinsically or in preferred order of implementation? Are all human rights reducible to a limited number of principles or is there little value in doing so? How are competing rights-claims to be adjudicated? What is the relationship between rights, needs and wants?

In view of such problems, some social thinkers question the value of using rights language at all, while others doubt the existence of human rights in the first place, not least because of how easy it is to manipulate rights to the advantage of those who deem them "self-evident."[11] But so entrenched is the concept in the modern mind, and such is the rhetorical power of appealing to rights, that most commentators believe it is an idea we cannot do without, despite its obscurities.

For our purposes, a broad definition of human rights, such as that given by Martin Shupack, is sufficient.

> Human rights are fundamental claims or entitlements that are acknowledged to be morally justified and that take precedence over other societal interests. Each person possesses the full panoply of human rights simply because he or she is a human being. Grounded in a belief in human dignity, human rights express the minimal requirements for human well-being.[12]

To have a right, then, is to have one's integrity and worth as a human being protected by the imposition of normative constraints, whether moral, legal or both. Rights represent legitimate claims on others, claims to have one's rights respected and provided for. Such rights exist, however, whether or not they are explicitly claimed by individuals; they are possessed simply in virtue of being human.[13]

THE EMERGENCE OF HUMAN RIGHTS

Linguistically the term *human rights* is of very recent vintage. It seems to have first been used toward the end of World

War II as an attempt by the Allies to articulate how what they stood for differed from the ideology of the Axis powers. With the founding of the United Nations Organization in 1945, the notion of human rights was consciously invoked as the basis for a new world order. The term supplanted the earlier phrase *natural rights*, which had fallen into disfavor partly because its foundational concept of natural law was considered empirically suspect. It also superseded the later phrase *the rights of man*, which could be understood to exclude the rights of women and children.

The origin of the human rights movement is as confusing and controversial as the meaning of the terminology itself. There are almost as many purported histories for human rights as there are historians, partly because it is not always clear whether commentators are talking about the *language* of rights, the *concept* of rights, *theories* of rights, the *practice* of rights, the notion of *legal* rights, or the specific idea of *human* rights.[14]

Rather than seeking a single tap root for human rights, it is probably wiser to think of a complex root system drawing on many different sources. The modern Western human rights doctrine represents a confluence of Greek philosophy, Roman legal practice, Judeo-Christian theological insights, and a range of philosophical ideas about individual liberty, scientific rationalism, and democratic humanism emanating from the Renaissance in Europe and the Enlightenment in Britain and America.

The immediate background of the modern doctrine lies in the flourishing of "natural rights" theories in the seventeenth and eighteenth centuries, which found expression in such documents as the American *Declaration of Independence* (1776), the French Assembly's *Declaration of the Rights of Man and of the Citizen* (1789), the American *Bill of Rights* (1789), and in Thomas Paine's work, *The Rights of Man* (1791). The concept of natural rights came under sustained philosophical and political attack from the late eighteenth-nineteenth centuries, and enjoyed little credence by the turn of the twentieth century. However the totalitarian assault on human dignity in the first half of the twentieth century, especially by Nazi Germany, Stalinist Russia and Imperialist Japan, led to the reinterpretation of traditional natural-rights doctrine in the direction of "human rights," together with an attempt to meet the criticisms leveled at natural rights theory.[15]

Several features of contemporary human rights theory remain philosophically problematic. But the vast majority of legal scholars, philosophers and moralists agree in principle with the existence of human rights, however defined and justified, not least because of the concept's usefulness in the struggle against oppression and injustice.

THE CONTENT OF HUMAN RIGHTS

Like all normative traditions, the human rights tradition reflects the processes of historical development and change. The French jurist Karel Vasak has identified three "generations" of human rights since the advent of modernity, each typified by one of the watchwords of the French Revolution: *liberté, égalite, fraternité.* Vasak's model is an over-simplification of the historical reality, but many experts find it helpful for bringing clarity to the debate over the content and scope of human rights.[16]

- First-generation rights comprise civil and political rights, derived primarily from the English, American and French revolutions of the seventeenth-eighteenth centuries. Fundamentally shaped by the political philosophy of liberal individualism and the social and economic doctrine of laissez-faire, such rights are largely negative in character— freedom from abuse and misuse by political authority. Belonging to the first generation are rights set forth in Articles 2-21 of UDHR, including the rights to life, liberty, and security of person; the rights not to be enslaved, tortured or to be subject to arbitrary arrest, detention, or exile; the right to privacy, freedom of thought, conscience, religion, movement, expression, assembly and association, and to a fair and public trial; the right to participate in government; the right to own property, and so on. The core concept of first generation rights is liberty, in particular the liberty of the individual from arbitrary state interference.
- Second-generation rights focus on economic, social and cultural rights, and find their origin in the socialist and

Marxist traditions of the nineteenth century, and in revolutionary and social welfare movements ever since. Reacting to the abuses of unrestrained, individualistic capitalism, second generation rights are more positive in character—"rights to" an equitable participation in, and benefit from, the production and distribution of wealth, secured through positive state intervention. A core concept of second generation rights is equality. The rights set forth in Articles 22-27 of the UDHR illustrate such rights, including the rights to work, to fair wages and to favorable working conditions; the right to rest and to periodic holidays with pay; the right to an adequate standard of living, to sufficient food, clothing, housing, health services and medical care; to social security in the event of unemployment, sickness, disability, widowhood and old age; the right to education; the right to take part in the cultural life of the community, and so on. States have a duty to seek the fullest possible realization of these rights up to the maximum of available resources.

• Third-generation rights, although foreshadowed in Article 28 of the UDHR, which proclaims that "everyone is entitled to a social and international order in which the rights set forth in this declaration can be realized," are a product of the anti-colonialist movement and the emergence of Third World nationalism. These so-called "solidarity" or "manifesto" rights include a demand for a global redistribution of wealth and power, the right to self-determination, the right to economic and social development, the right to an equal share in the earth's resources, and the rights to peace, a healthy environment and to disaster relief. All such rights are collective or fraternity rights, requiring the co-operation of societal and political institutions on a global scale to secure their effecting, although an individual dimension is also implied.

In more recent discussion, especially in ecumenical Christian circles, reference is also found to fourth- and fifth- generation rights. Fourth-generation rights focus on environmental or ecological rights, or, better expressed, human responsibilities toward the environment (i.e., the right of the environment to human care). Fifth- or "future generation" rights center on the rights of unborn generations to share the resources and benefits of the earth. Whether such concerns really represent a distinct category of rights is debatable. It is perhaps preferable to view them as developments within third-generation rights (although the extension of the notion to rights to non-human creation and unborn humans raises special problems).[17]

Now the categories of second-, third-, and further-generation rights have been the source of considerable controversy. Although most nations of the world have endorsed both the *International Covenant on Civil and Political Rights* (1966) and the *International Covenant on Economic, Social and Cultural Rights* (1976), arguments over the relative priority of each category were common during the Cold War and are still heard today in discussions between wealthy and developing nations.

First World countries tend to argue that civil and political rights are an essential prerequisite for social justice and economic development, and are therefore deserving of primary emphasis. Two-Thirds-World governments, on the other hand, sometimes see civil and political rights as a luxury they cannot afford before achieving economic and social transformation. The primary human right in their situation is the right to live and to eat, the right to be free from the legacy of colonial exploitation and imposed poverty. Socialist regimes, like China, subordinate individual rights to the rights of the state to enjoy political stability, and see the pressure from Western democracies for individual human rights as a form of cultural imperialism.

Another area of controversy concerns the wisdom of extending the notion of rights to include social and economic goals.[18] Some commentators argue that it is wiser to limit the term human rights to those entitlements whose universality is most clearly recognized in moral discourse, such as the right to liberty or life, which every moral community can recognize. By contrast there are such significant differences of opinion over cultural, economic, and environmental concerns that it is hard to see how they can be regarded as self-evident rights.

Critics point out that the items included in the second and third generations are better understood as needs, social ideals, and aspirations rather than rights. To term them rights, they insist, violates the semantic conventions that normally govern the word. In everyday usage, a right is something possessed by a person or group to prevent interference from others, not something that specifies ends or ideals.

Another distinguishing feature is that a right carries a correlative duty for some agency to deliver the right. In principle, negative rights can be enforced. But it is extremely difficult to suggest how the delivery of positive social and economic rights can be enforced, or even to specify which party can be held accountable for doing so. How are impoverished nations to satisfy such rights as allowing every person title to property, choice of gainful employment, holidays with pay, education, health care, and old-age security?

The effect of branding such ideals as "rights," critics maintain, is to detract from the moral power of other human rights assertions. All human rights talk is pushed out of the realm of the morally compelling and into the twilight zone of utopian aspirations. It also leads to the tragic paradox of a world community that is still unable to prevent the grossest violations of human rights, such as genocide and child prostitution, yet persists in transposing every worthy cause or human good into an international "right."

The opposite point is made by defenders of second- and third-generation rights. So important are matters like basic health care, adequate educational opportunities, and decent employment conditions for the achievement of human potential and the creation of a humane society, they argue, there is every justification for casting them in the rhetorically persuasive idiom of human rights. Moreover, without minimal standards in health, food and education, civil and political liberties cannot be nurtured or protected. To term social and cultural aspirations "rights" also avoids paternalism. It serves to empower the disadvantaged by acknowledging the legitimacy of their claims to be free of dehumanizing deprivation and oppression.

Supporters of the practice also point out that the distinction between positive and negative rights is not absolute. Such negative rights as the right to security of the person, freedom from arbitrary arrest, and participation in government, cannot be assured without affirmative government action. On the other hand, several positive rights, such as the right to form trade unions or the right to participate in the cultural life of the community, do not necessarily depend on affirmative state action.

In the historical evolution of the human rights tradition, then, two interesting developments have occurred. One is the terminological shift that has taken place over time from natural *law* to natural *rights* to *human* rights; the other is the progressive widening of the meaning of *rights* to include social ideals, goals and aspirations in addition to enforceable legal or moral claims and entitlements. Second- and third- generation rights have more to do with aspirations than justice. The virtue of terming them "rights" lies in their implied obligations. These include seeking the common good domestically and fostering peace and development internationally, not out of charity or pity or enlightened self-interest but in recognition of the common humanity and common entitlements of all peoples, as well as the ultimate interdependence of individual, communal and ecological well-being.[19]

The weakness in deeming them "rights" lies in the semantic overloading of rights language and in the impossibility of holding any party specifically accountable for the delivery of such wide-ranging claims. Philosophically the category of rights has become more ambiguous and difficult to define, with obvious implications for political implementation. Also the increasing practice of bringing situations of markedly different gravity within the orbit of human rights risks trivialization of the idea itself. To defend access to pornography or the withholding of school reports from parents in terms of human rights surely diminishes the moral power of the concept. As rights language proliferates and becomes increasingly bizarre, the less useful it becomes in resolving moral disagreements.

On the other hand there remains something vitally important, even irreplaceable, about the notion of human rights. It is better able than any equivalent phrase to give voice to certain essential convictions about the worth of human life, the nature of human relationships, and the limits of state power. For this reason, most contemporary social thinkers are reluctant to push their analysis of the theoretical and semantic shortcomings of rights-talk to the point of overtly repudiating the concept itself. Life is larger than logic, and the advantages associated with employing the notion of human rights far outweigh the disadvantages.

UNIVERSAL RIGHTS AND CULTURAL RELATIVISM

The notion of human rights implies a universal conception of what is "human" and what is "right." It entails, as Max Stackhouse notes, "the implicit assertion that certain principles are true and valid for all peoples, in all societies, under all conditions of economic, political, ethnic, and cultural life. Further, human rights implies that these principles are somehow present in the very fact of our common humanity, properly understood."[20] In other words, for something to be deemed a human right it must, by definition, apply to every human being, irrespective of race, class, age, sex, religion, historical location or any other distinction. It is a universal ethic that ought to be believed and observed by everyone everywhere.

In recent years, however, controversy has arisen over whether human rights canons are truly universal or are merely Western cultural values masquerading as universal principles. A number of factors have contributed to the emergence of this debate. One factor has been the popular legacy of the doctrine of cultural relativism, which flourished in cultural anthropology in the 1930s. Cultural relativism rejects the possibility of there being universal moral standards because the articulation and justification of any such standards is inevitably culturally based, and therefore relative. Different norms apply to different cultures, and to different stages or forms of social organization. Criteria for understanding and evaluating a culture remain relative to that culture.

This logically applies as much to human rights standards as to any other cultural norms.[21] All formulations of human rights are historically contingent and socially conditioned; they are not natural or divine givens. Even the UDHR mirrors concerns of its own age and embodies the asymmetry of political power that prevailed in the immediate post-war period.

Such awareness of the conditionedness of human rights statements and theories, combined with a general reluctance to critique one culture's practices on the basis of the values and insights treasured by another, has made assertions of universality for human rights problematic. China, Indonesia, and several other Asian countries have seized on this fact to defend their own human rights record from Western criticism. They have argued that Western definitions are not appropriate to Asian circumstances and that it is culturally more appropriate for the collective rights of the state to take priority over individual civil and political rights.

The hypocrisy and selective morality of Western nations has strengthened their case. While criticizing developing countries for human rights abuses, Western nations have continued to trade in the most inhumane weapons of mass destruction, to turn a blind eye to the crimes of pro-Western tyrants, and to oversee a global economic order that brings untold misery to the world's poorest people. As Felix Wilfred comments,

> One cannot but wonder whether the human rights system has not become an instrument in the hands of the self-righteous, powerful nations of the West to bully the poor nations of the Third World and continue unabated their economic and political hegemony. . . . The indictment of a third-world country for violation of human rights often means it refuses to play the games of market economy according to the rules framed by the West.[22]

Such an alignment of human rights rhetoric with sectional Western interests throws into question the universal validity of the human rights principles championed by the West.

Another factor contributing to the problem has been the loss of confidence, in postmodern thought and culture, in the capacity of reason to discover universal moral norms or objective "foundations" on which to build systems of truth. The usual basis for asserting the universality of human rights within the Western secular human rights tradition has consequently been eroded. Where Enlightenment modernity championed reason over revelation, postmodernity asserts fragmentation and relativism over reason.

Some postmodern thinkers insist that any claim to define universal moral norms or to make grand truth claims for any meta-narrative is inherently and inescapably oppressive, since it requires the exclusion or denial of alternative viewpoints and the marginalization of groups that hold them. Rather than seeking universal moral standards or metaphysical truths, people must claim the right to define such truth and morality for themselves, and *only* for themselves.

Such skepticism toward the metaphysical basis for truth and morality makes the postmodern situation historically unique, contends Duncan Forrester. In the past societies have gone through similar periods of uncertainty about the meaning of morality and justice as we are experiencing today. What is new is the rejection of any belief in an objective grounding for truth and "the enthusiasm with which many thinkers embrace pluralism and a kind of moral relativism as if this were an achievement rather than a predicament."[23] In postmodernity, then, contextual sensitivity and a fascination with personal entitlements and self-defining moral autonomy have undermined belief in those moral absolutes and transcendental ethical norms upon which human rights assertions have traditionally rested.

In response, it may be noted that the problem of making and legitimating universal truth claims in an environment of cultural diversity and moral relativism is a very real one. It is a familiar problem to Christian theologians and apologists, and it confronts everyone engaged in international human rights work as well. It is true that all moral statements are unavoidably contextual in nature and that all existing human rights statements are bound to particular times and places. But if this means there are no universal standards which humans can know and use as a basis for intercultural judgments, albeit imperfectly, the door is left open for all manner of abuses to be justified in the name of cultural distinction. A thoroughgoing consideration to this dilemma is not possible here but some initial comments on the epistemological, moral, and empirical difficulties with cultural relativism may be made.

Epistemological considerations

The first thing to say is that recognizing the contingent character of human moral constructs is not the same as saying they are *entirely* or *absolutely* contingent. The main problem with cultural (or moral) relativism is, ironically, that it falsely absolutizes a relative truth. Cultural and moral criteria *are* contextually conditioned; to that extent relativism is real. But to move from that empirical observation to the normative assertion that "all things are entirely relative" is epistemologically self-defeating, since the conclusion itself must be an exception to the proposition of total relativism.

A similar antinomy dogs the rejection of all "foundations" in philosophical discourse or literary theory in favor of wholly consensual or radically contingent theories of truth.[24] The antifoundational starting point itself becomes an incipient foundation, the first principle upon which the denial of first principles takes place. Furthermore, assertions of radical contingency are frequently justified on the basis of rational and evidential arguments even though reason and evidence are dismissed as contingent and unstable. In the long run, then, antifoundationalism risks self-destruction by creating and defending foundations in the process of rejecting them.[25]

The same observation applies to the values often used to commend cultural and moral relativism, such as the need for tolerance, modesty, freedom, and mutual respect. To appeal to such values to justify relativism either means that these values are being treated as supracultural or universal truths, which relativists deny in principle, or else the moral values of Western liberalism are being used as the basis for approaching all other cultures—which is intolerant, immodest, coercive, and disrespectful since it disallows any culture to make absolute truth claims for its own viewpoint (as nearly every culture does) simply because such claims transgress Western liberal assumptions. Accordingly, if it is possible (indeed necessary) to make absolute assertions about and in favor of relativism, then in principle it must also be possible to make absolute assertions about and in favor of human rights.

To admit that human rights principles are historically conditioned is not to say that their truthfulness is exhausted by those historical circumstances or that they are inapplicable to other, markedly different, historical and cultural conditions. There is no reason why one could not accept the relativity of moral statements (in the sense of acknowledging the provisional and contextual character of all human knowledge) while at the same time insisting that, given what we know about the human condition, they still apply to all known human situations. Rather than setting up sterile and simplistic dichotomies between relative/absolute or local/universal, it is better to imagine a continuum with some moral values situated nearer the local/relative pole and others, such as core human rights values, falling nearer the universal/absolute pole.

Of course, all determinations of what should be located near to each pole are themselves unavoidably contextual. The universals distilled in Western experience may not necessarily accord with the universals identified in non-Western societies. Moreover, as Wilfred points out, the very meaning of the concept *universal* differs from culture to culture. In the Western tradition, universals have typically been understood as abstract properties that transcend, and hence subordinate, all concrete, particular or local expressions. This understanding tends toward domination, both because it fails to recognize its own partisan conceptual character and because it seeks to conform all local expressions to a universal (Western) standard.

But in India, and in much of the Two-Thirds World, Wilfred explains, the notion of universal is inextricably bound up with context. The particular is an integral part of the universal. In a way, it *is* the universal manifest in everyday experience. From this perspective it follows that basic *human needs*— the need for food, shelter, security, social relationships and so on—are most naturally seen as universal human rights.[26]

What all this means is that to recognize the inescapably contextual nature of existing human rights definitions is not to invalidate any possibility of them bearing universal validity. At the same time, it suggests that universals cannot successfully be imposed on local situations from without but must emerge from within, or eventually be validated by, particular cultures, religions and histories.

Moral considerations

Thoroughgoing cultural relativism is also morally dangerous. If questions of truth are not involved in human rights
claims but only questions of cultural acceptability, in the final
analysis, might makes right.[27] No ultimate answer can be
given to the question, "Why not be cruel?" No moral objections can be raised to the exclusion of whole groups of people
from any claim to human rights so long as that exclusion is
consistent with the reigning cultural understandings of the
majority. Practices like female genital mutilation might out-
rage *our* sense of propriety, but we could offer no persuasive
argument for why such a practice ought not to be followed
within cultural settings that approve of it.

If moral truth is grounded merely in the prevailing consensus of particular communities at particular times, there are
no grounds for saying Hitler was wrong if the majority of Germans believed he was right. If the quest for transcendent
norms is to be rejected as inherently oppressive, and cultural
diversity and moral autonomy are to be embraced as final
goods in themselves, no adequate basis exists for adjudicating
the claims of competing communities or for rejecting the freely
chosen behavior of any group, even if it is destructive of themselves or of others. Consensual theories of truth and goodness
ultimately require silence in the face of evil committed by
those in other communities with a different consensus.

The fact that some of the most repressive regimes in the
world today appeal to cultural values to resist conformity to
human rights conventions is a sign of the moral price to be
paid for absolutizing culture and relativizing morality. Assertions of universalism may mask Western imperialism, but
easy-going relativism can equally become the last refuge of repression.[28] This is why recent human rights documents, such
as the *Vienna Declaration* (1993), acknowledge "the significance
of national and regional particularities" (par. 5) but still insist
on the universal nature of human rights and freedoms.

Empirical considerations

Cultural relativism is also empirically dubious. The degree of universality or relativity in moral and cultural values

is an empirical question, capable of demonstration. Certainly the extent of diversity between cultures is impressive. But commonalities also exist, and especially in areas related to fundamental human rights. It appears that all cultures recognize a distinction between the human and the non-human; human solidarity is itself a kind of primal objectivity. All human societies seek to distinguish between good and evil; all employ language and rationality (hence crosscultural communication and comparison are possible);[29] all societies condemn unjustified killing, betrayal, kidnapping, stealing, and slander; all affirm values of faithfulness, honesty, and sacrifice.

Such categories are sometimes given different ethical content, and they fulfill different functions within an overall religio-ethical framework. But beneath the different forms of expression often lie similar moral perceptions, and whether the divergences of expression make it impossible to arrive at crosscultural agreement on basic human rights is doubtful. Although the UDHR cannot be said to function as a universal moral standard, its legal universality at least tells in favor of the intelligibility of its assertions across cultural and political divides. Similarly, while repressive regimes appeal to relativism to deflect Western criticism, human rights activists within those countries, operating within the same cultural universe as their leaders, affirm and demand allegedly "Western" conceptions of individual rights as their own.

This is not to say that we can arrive at a comprehensive definition of universal human rights simply by identifying areas of agreement between the world's religions and cultures.[30] To limit definitions of rights to those core values all agree on would fail to address issues of underlying anthropology and would be so general as to be of limited value in implementing specific provisions. All might agree on the right to life, for example, but disagree on when life commences and in what circumstances it is right to terminate it.

Perhaps a more promising strategy would be for different cultural and religious communities to construct their own edifices of human rights, based on their own local traditions and beliefs, and for these more detailed accounts to become the basis for interreligious dialogue and mutual crosscultural critique. Common ground would emerge and differences could be debated, in the hope that what is most true to human experience would ultimately be vindicated.[31] Crosscultural critique is not easy or risk free. But the effort must still be made, both because evaluative judgments cannot be avoided in life and because "human rights suffer as much by timidity as by dogmatic and arrogant ethnocentrism in making normative judgments."[32]

Certainly Christians should welcome such dialogue. It would allow the distinctiveness of the Christian voice to be heard; it would require Western secularism to concede its own limited contextual (and religious) character; and it would represent a peacemaking approach to issues of cultural conflict. Far from diluting the truth claims of Christian faith, it would invite the consideration and testing of them, along with the truth claims of all other religions and philosophies.

Biblical and Christian tradition has always assumed there are universal principles of justice and morality that apply to all peoples on earth and that are at least partly knowable by all (through natural revelation or natural law). If Christian faith represents the clearest expression of the Creator's will, then any agreement that emerges from international conversation on human rights will be congruent with Christian conceptions of the good life.[33]

Conversely, if Christian claims are true, then Christianity will prove itself to be a better basis for developing universal human rights than any of its alternatives. It will only do so by offering a deeper grasp of human nature, a better basis for making reliable crosscultural judgments and implementing human rights in various social contexts while respecting local diversity, and a more compelling account of metaphysical reality than any of its rivals.

But to what extent is the concept congenial to Christian faith? What relationship does it bear to the assumptions and teachings of the Bible? In the next chapter I will briefly explore the connection between human rights and Christian tradition, then in the following chapters focus specifically on the biblical story itself.

2
Christian Faith and Human Rights

Iᴛ ɪs ᴍʏ ᴄᴏɴᴛᴇɴᴛɪᴏɴ ɪɴ ᴛʜɪs ʙᴏᴏᴋ ᴛʜᴀᴛ Christian faith, informed by the biblical tradition, has something distinctive to say about human rights, something that enriches and, at points, corrects the approach to human rights that prevails in the Western secular tradition.

However, this is a controversial claim. In a secular context, the validity or value of seeking to relate human rights to religious beliefs is not self-evident. Even within theological discussion, there is disagreement on whether a Christian account of human rights is substantially different to a secular account. Equally controversial is how the biblical text is best appropriated for Christian reflection on the subject. "The line from the Bible to human rights," James Barr observes, "is not a straight or an easy one."[34] Before turning to the biblical text, a word should be said about each of these matters.

IS A RELIGIOUS PERSPECTIVE VALID?

Objections to the attempt to relate human rights to Christian faith come from both inside and outside the church. Within the church, many conservative Christians look with great suspicion on any talk of rights, deeming it to be humanistic, egotistical, and overly optimistic about human nature. Human beings, they insist, are sinners; they have no rights before God, least of all absolute and inalienable rights. The fact that most human rights declarations make no mention of God, and that people appeal to rights to justify licentious lifestyles, simply confirms that rights have nothing to do with divine revelation. They are an expression of human rebellion against the law of God, a law which makes demands, not issues rights.

A different kind of objection comes from outside the church. In a society where secularism is the officially sanctioned basis of public life and religion is confined to the private realm, attempts to build a human rights doctrine on explicit religious presuppositions may be discounted on two main grounds.

First, there is a widespread feeling that religious beliefs and practices are more often a factor in the infringement of human rights than in their promotion and defense. Religious adherents normally claim privileged status for their beliefs and practices, an attitude which encourages intolerance toward outsiders. Religious rivalries sometimes flare up into violent conflicts entailing gross violations of human rights. The track record of institutional Christianity in this respect speaks for itself. Historically the church has exercised temporal and spiritual authority in a way that has disregarded human aspirations to freedom, oppressed minorities, and curtailed or denied freedom of expression.[35]

Second, there is the common assumption that whereas the secular language of rights is ideologically neutral and universal in scope, religious discourse is local and ideologically partisan. In the wake of the Enlightenment, the tradition-neutral language of rights was intended to supersede the parochial moral discourse of determinate religious communities. After all, if human rights are possessed by every human being, their authority and intelligibility cannot be made dependent on the world view of limited and diverse religious communities. Human rights must rest on something more universal, something which transcends all provincial, group-specific norms—namely, enlightened human reason.

What can be said in response to such objections? To begin with, it would be unfair to construe the influence of religion on human rights in wholly negative terms. Religious traditions are deeply ambiguous and complex phenomena, giving expression to the best as well as the worst in human nature.[36]

This is certainly true of the Christian tradition. The Church has been guilty of the most awful crimes against humanity, but it has also done much to foster belief in the equality of every individual before God and to encourage powerful works of charity and justice-making. In many parts of the world today, the Christian church is one of the most influential forces in the human rights struggle, due both to its closeness to ordinary people and to its extensive international links.

The particularity of religious discourse must be conceded. But the assumption that stating human rights principles in secular terms enhances their universal currency is itself intensely ethnocentric and parochial. Secularism is still a predominantly Western phenomenon, encapsulating a worldview alien to much of the world's population. Even in the West, secularism is by no means universal.[37] The increasing ethnic and cultural pluralism of most Western countries means that secularism exists side by side with a diversity of alternative world views.

How best to promote the universal validity of human rights in face of such diversity is certainly problematic. But the Enlightenment belief that it is possible to identify universal moral standards independent of particular moral and cultural traditions is false. The discourse on rights does not occur in neutral space, based on value-free reasoning. "For there is no place which is not some place in particular and there are no reasons that are not reasons for someone."[38] By remaining oblivious to its own parochialism, and by failing to take into account the importance of religious convictions, Western secularism may even be counter-productive to the acceptance of human rights in other cultures.[39]

By contrast, the conscious attempt to root human rights in religious belief has potential for strengthening respect for human rights. The greatest safeguard for human rights lies in having human rights convictions thoroughly integrated in the moral psychology of a people and connected to its deepest convictions about the meaning of human life. Religion is better equipped to do this than are the structures of the secular state. Christian faith in particular aims to write God's law on the human heart and to nurture the values and qualities of character necessary for human rights to flourish.[40]

Religious belief is also more able to motivate people to seek human rights. One of the most effective ways to inspire people to pursue high moral ideals is to relate them to religious conceptions about the good life. As John Clayton observes, "in comparison to the image of the good life projected in the authoritative texts of many religions, the narrowly secular discourse of rights looks decidedly thin."[41]

At the end of the day, it is impossible to avoid religious considerations in any discussion of human rights. Both the French *Déclaration des droits de l'homme* (1789) and the American *Declaration of Independence* (1776) recognize that political bodies do not create or grant rights; they "recognize" and "proclaim" them. The American Declaration expressly mentions the divine origin of human rights: all men are equal because they are *created* equal and *endowed* with rights by their *Creator*. The French declaration substitutes "nature" for the Creator: all men are *born* with equal rights, and these are of *nature*. That these rights are pronounced "sacred" shows that a religious background is still operative.

The same applies to modern statements. When the preamble to the Universal Declaration of Human Rights "proclaims" the existence, universality, and absolute value of human rights, it is making assertions of faith, based on a particular understanding of human existence, and is hence inherently religious in character. The obligation it enjoins on "every individual and every organ of society" to "keep the Declaration constantly in mind" and to strive by "teaching and education to promote respect for these rights and freedoms" is powerfully reminiscent on the Torah's injunction to lay up God's words "in your heart and soul," to "bind them . . . on your hand and fix them . . . on your forehead," and constantly to "teach them to your children" (Deut. 11:18-20).

Article 1 states that all human beings are born free and equal in dignity and rights. Not only is this a religious assertion, it is one that stands in tension with certain other religious anthropologies, such as those that believe human existence is determined by the *karma* accrued in previous lives, so that people are *not* born equal in dignity, rights and freedom. In its dependence on an ultimate metaphysical-moral vision of what is meaningful and what values and relationships are sacrosanct, the UDHR may fairly be depicted as "a 'creedal articulation,' religious in root and branch."[42]

The choice, then, ultimately is not between a religious or a non-religious approach to human rights but between *explicitly* religious conceptions of human rights and *implicitly* religious conceptions. Human rights cannot exist simply as a set of isolated positivist demands. To be meaningful, such demands depend on a larger world view, an overarching interpretation of human nature and human existence.

Inasmuch as it furnishes such an interpretation, secularism is a de facto religion, one that refuses to admit its own religious character. More than that, secularism is a stepchild of Christianity. The secular human rights tradition was forged on the foundation of Christian theological assumptions and a Christian value system that encouraged respect for individual dignity. The accumulated capital of that Christian ethic is now substantially depleted in Western culture, which makes consideration of a Christian perspective on human rights timely as well as legitimate.

THE DIVERSITY OF CHRISTIAN APPROACHES

There is, however, no such thing as a single Christian perspective on human rights. Different theological traditions have adopted different approaches to defining and explaining human rights. The Roman Catholic church has traditionally approached human rights within a "nature-grace" framework. Human dignity and human rights derive from nature but are confirmed and made clearer in the gospel of Christ. Accordingly, the concepts of natural law and universal reason are invoked as the primary basis for the existence and universality of human rights.[43]

The Lutheran tradition has employed its typical "two kingdoms" schema for apprehending human rights. Viewed through this lense, human rights are secular norms belonging to the realm of law and illuminated by reason rather than by distinctively Christian norms belonging to the realm of gospel.[44] Human rights thus lack a uniquely Christian foundation, although Christian analogies exist and the gospel motivates Christians to work for justice and empowers them to exceed the minimal levels achievable in the world.

The Reformed tradition, together with many non-conformist churches, grounds human rights in the sphere of redemption.[45] Human rights are not given in the laws of nature but gifted by God in creation and covenant relation. It is only by means of Christian revelation that human rights can be accurately known and fully respected (though common grace enables some discernment of human rights by unbelievers).

Liberation theology, including feminist theology, begins with the common human experience of oppression and links human rights to the praxis of liberation, to which the gospel also calls us.[46] Liberationist thought is deeply sensitive to the extent to which traditional formulations of human rights manifest Western capitalist or androcentric assumptions and seeks to construct more inclusive and representative formulations.

As well as employing different theological frameworks, different approaches are taken by Christian thinkers to grasping and articulating the diversity of human rights. One common approach is to identify a limited number of fundamental principles that underlie all human rights, such as freedom, equality, solidarity, life, dignity, and so on. Another approach is to locate the unity of human rights in the singular concept of human dignity and to explain the plurality of rights as outworkings of that dignity.

The significance of such diversity of Christian perspectives should not be overestimated, however. The various frameworks employed are not mutually exclusive, even if they differ in emphasis. Moreover analysis of the major ecumenical statements on human rights reveals remarkable commonalties of concern.[47]

Two further features unite Christian reflection on human rights. One is its relatively peripheral status in mainstream theological discussion, which is symptomatic perhaps of a larger retreat by Christians thinkers from social engagement. As Duncan Forrester observes,

> Western academic theology seems to have largely abandoned serious addressing of questions of justice, and it no longer appears to know how to engage in secular debate

about the nature of justice. . . . Academic theology to a dis-
tressing degree has *chosen* to withdraw from social issues,
and is willingly confined to a private world, where it nurtures a pervasive uncertainty about its role and function,
an uncertainty which incapacitates it from making the kind
of powerful contribution to the debate about justice which
Barth, Brunner and Reinhold Niebuhr did two generations
ago.[48]

The other common feature is more positive. It is the conviction that the witness of the Christian Scriptures to the creative and redemptive activity of God offers a unique horizon
for understanding human rights. Even in Catholic and
Lutheran approaches, which tend to locate human rights
norms outside of Christian revelation, substantial recourse is
made to the biblical text to confirm and clarify such norms. All
theological traditions agree that the Bible has a crucial, though
not exclusive, role to play in Christian ethical reflection. Having said that, the best way to relate the Scriptures to human
rights remains problematic for all traditions.[49]

THE USE AND LIMITS OF THE BIBLE

In approaching the Bible for help in constructing a Christian account of human rights, interpreters face specific problems. The first is determining whether the Bible even refers to
human rights. Opinion is divided. Some writers assert boldly
that "The Bible is a proclamation of universal human rights"[50]
and that "Human rights are clearly set down in the law of
Moses."[51] Others insist that neither the terminology nor the
contemporary notion of human rights appears anywhere in
the biblical text; "the only self-evident right in the Bible is the
sovereign right of God over creation and creatures."[52]

Certainly texts can be found to match every right listed in
the Universal Declaration of Human Rights.[53] However, several scholars warn of the danger of anachronism and distortion in attaching the term *human rights* to biblical teaching,
since there are major differences between the presuppositions
of key biblical prescriptions and modern human rights canons.

Elaine Pagels argues, for example, that throughout antiquity, and in Western society up until the Enlightenment, as

well as in all traditional societies, Eastern and Western, rights derive not from conceptions of inherent dignity but from membership in society. Possession of rights is determined by one's place in the social order, which is believed to reflect the divine order. Leaders can therefore make claims on others which cannot be made on them by others because leaders rule by divine right.[54]

James Barr also points to "a striking difference in terms of approach and expression" between modern human rights discourse and moral discourse in Scripture. The Bible's moral imperatives are *theonomous* (framed as personal commands from God); in human rights theory, moral claims are *anthroponomous* (they attach intrinsically to the human person). The Bible focuses on the responsibility of actors to do no wrong; human rights focuses on people being protected from the wrongdoing of others. In the Bible, ultimate value attaches to divine commandment; in human rights it attaches to human freedom. Biblical law and teaching are intended only for the covenant community; human rights apply to everyone.[55]

Other scholars note further contrasts. Human rights doctrine employs abstract categories; biblical thought displays "an overwhelming preference for concrete and particular formulations over the general and the abstract."[56] Human rights documents proclaim ideals; biblical documents describe, and sometimes prescribe, standards of behavior that fall short of ideals. Human rights speaks of the inherent value of the individual; biblical thought finds the idea of human existence outside the family/tribe inconceivable and assumes that individual needs will yield in precedence to the rights and needs of the family.[57] Human rights stresses personal autonomy, popular sovereignty, and legitimate claims on government; the Bible disapproves of people doing "what is right in their own eyes" (Judg. 17:6), invests true governing authority in God, and stresses obligations over rights.[58]

In view of such differences, it would be futile to look for a fully blown human rights doctrine in the Bible, employing a range of legal, moral, or philosophical concepts similar to those used today. Most scholars suggest that the relationship between Scripture and human rights is oblique or indirect.

The relationship is nonetheless real. There *are* places in the biblical text where a conception of rights appears. There *are* provisions in biblical law that presuppose the equal dignity of all human beings and issue in benefits parallel to human rights. There *are* fundamental values, beliefs, and concerns that bear deep affinity with modern human rights thought.[59]

Most important, there is an overarching narrative structure of Creation-Fall-Redemption-Consummation, fleshed out in teaching on God's righteousness and the covenantal nature of community, that has sweeping implications of a human-rights kind. "The deepest roots of human rights," Max Stackhouse asserts, "are found in the biblical conception of life. The words 'human rights' do not, to be sure, appear in the Bible, but the themes that provide the basis of human rights do."[60]

A second problem lies in dealing with the ambiguity of the biblical witness. On the one hand, the Bible offers the most profound conception of human personhood and sanctity ever conceived. On the other, it appears to mandate such human rights abuses as slavery, war, conquest, genocide, the subjugation of women, bridal sale, racial separation, the denial of religious freedom to idolaters, and the execution of wrongdoers. Because of this ambiguity, "the same biblical material that has inspired the quest for social justice has been appealed to and used as an instrument for rejecting that quest."[61]

Such ambiguity indicates a certain tension in the biblical record between ideal and reality, or between theory and practice, with respect to human rights.[62] Theologically this tension may be explained by the reality of sin in the world, which imposed constraints on the extent to which the full implications of human rights could be realized in any given historical situation (cf. Mark 10:5).

This means that in using the Bible, we ought to give preference to its deepest and most pervasive themes relating to human worth, while acknowledging the contingent or historical nature of the concrete outworking of those themes in the history of Israel and the church. We must beware of too quickly condemning ancient practices on the basis of modern sensitivities—as though had *we* lived in the ancient world, *we* would have done things differently!

In addition, we need to remember that sometimes hidden within the very institutions and practices which seem inimical to modern human rights definitions, there were values acknowledged, or humanizing factors at work, which derived from a high view of human worth and which functioned historically as leaven for change in the direction of greater humanization (see further below).

A third difficulty is determining how best to bridge the cultural, historical, and religious chasm between the worlds of the Bible and today. This is a problem that confronts biblical interpreters every time they consult the text for moral guidance. There is no space to explore this issue in detail here, but two recurring emphases in recent scholarship offer significant help.

One is the new appreciation scholars have today for the basic importance of the Bible's *narrative* material for ethical reflection. Traditionally primacy has been given to abstract concepts or underlying principles reified from the text, with the narrative material being discarded once the appropriate concept is identified. Today many would agree with Richard Hays that narrative texts are fundamental resources for normative ethics, "more fundamental than any secondary process of abstraction that seeks to distill their ethical import."[63]

It is not only the narrative genre within the Bible that is important but also the narrative *function* of the Bible as a whole. Human beings characteristically give expression to their understanding of life and the world in narrative form. Human communities are founded on shared traditions, the irreducible core of which is a shared story which cannot be demythologized into abstract ideas or directives. For the Christian community, it is the biblical story of God's creative and redemptive activity that furnishes its shared narrative, its source of identity. And it is this story that represents the real Christian contribution to the debate of human rights.[64]

In the past, Christian thinkers have often sought to contribute to public discussion of moral and political issues by translating Christian values into "middle axioms," an ethical "Esperanto" acceptable in the public square.[65] But Christian values—including those related to human rights—make most sense in light of the Christian story, and often it is that story that gives even common-sense values a distinctive flavor.

The other emphasis involves the *paradigmatic function* of biblical texts in informing Christian ethics.[66] A paradigm is something used as a model or example for other cases, where the basic principles or concerns remain unchanged although details differ. Paradigms are not to be imitated, but applied creatively. Each application will be different, but when necessary adjustments are made, each will conform to the essential principles, values, or convictions at work in the paradigm.

Both Israel and the New Testament churches were intended to function as a "light to the nations" (Isa. 42:6; Matt. 5:14-15). Rather than trying to replicate the laws and institutions of these communities today, we should seek to discern the structure of values and beliefs behind them. Then, in "an integrative act of metaphorical imagination" (Hays), we need to find ways to embody such values and beliefs in analogous institutions today. With respect to human rights, a paradigmatic approach allows us to use different aspects of the life of Israel and the church to inform, critique, and create human rights practices and convictions in our own age.

With these two ideas in mind, I turn now to consider the biblical tradition. My treatment cannot, of course, be exhaustive. My strategy will be to focus on several key narrative moments in the larger biblical story or acts in the biblical drama. Each time I will be seeking to discern values and beliefs that have implications for human rights and where possible making comparisons with contemporary thought.

This means my approach will be more than descriptive or historical. It will necessarily entail a degree of theological interpretation and appropriation of specific texts in light of their larger canonical setting, an analysis of key passages or themes from the perspective of a particular, faith-based construal of the direction and meaning of the overall biblical story.

That story, I suggest, has six main "moments" with human rights significance: Creation, Cultural Mandate, Covenant, Christ, Church, and Consummation. Though not necessarily in equal depth, I will explore each of these in turn in the chapters that follow.

3

Creation: Human Rights Originate in Creation

SINCE THE ENLIGHTENMENT, THE TERM *DIGNITY* has been used to express the fundamental worth of being human. Dignity is best thought of not as a right but as the source and justification for all human rights. Human rights in turn express entitlement to human dignity. Within the secular human rights tradition of Western liberal society, human dignity is either asserted as an *a priori* or is grounded in such distinctively human capacities as rationality, self-awareness, or moral consciousness.

Secular theory is most vulnerable at this point of justifying human dignity. It is either unable to explain why it exists, or else it links dignity to certain functions, most of which, as animal rights activists are quick to point out, have analogies in the animal world, and some of which are lacking in certain human beings (e.g., unborn children, infants, the mentally impaired, sociopaths). "The doctrine of individual rights bears the weight of the liberal edifice," Robert Gascoigne observes, "yet is itself quite often bereft of support, suspended in a metaphysical vacuum."[67]

Many social theorists today insist that human worth in liberal societies cannot be grounded on any metaphysical speculations or religious beliefs, since such beliefs or speculations are not accessible to all citizens. Gascoigne offers a sophisticated argument, however, for the importance of public ethics in liberal societies being undergirded by an ontology of the human person to prevent impoverishing the very values essential to the functioning of liberal society itself.

The greatest strength of a biblically based human rights ethic lies in its capacity to show how human dignity and its associated rights have a metaphysical raison d'être. Both are grounded in the creative and redemptive activity of God.

THE IMAGE OF GOD

In the biblical creation narratives, human dignity is demonstrated both by the *place* of human beings in the order of creation and by the *manner* of their creation. In Genesis 1, the creation of humankind is not just last in a series of creative acts; it serves as the goal of God's entire creative intention. After ordering the cosmos and creating the earth in such a way as to be capable of sustaining human life (cf. vv. 28-30), God announces his intention to create humankind.

Unlike other ancient Near Eastern creation myths, the biblical accounts are geocentric and anthropocentric in focus, placing a "concern with human life and the lives of humans at the very center of religious concern."[68] As the height of God's creative activity, human beings ought never to be considered mere instruments for some "higher" end. Each person is an end in himself or herself. And the reason for this lies in the *manner* of human creation, for humans alone are created in the image of God.

> Then God said, "Let us make humankind in our image, according to our likeness; and let them have dominion over the fish of the sea, and over the birds of the air, and over the cattle, and over all the wild animals of the earth, and over every creeping thing that creeps upon the earth." So God created humankind in his image, in the image of God he created them; male and female he created them. (Gen. 1:26-27; cf. 2:7; 5:1-2; 9:6)

There has long been debate over what precisely it means to be made in God's image.[69] Suggestions have ranged from physical resemblance to God, through possession of intelligence, free will, imagination, and conscience; to autonomy and sexuality. But rather than reducing the image of God to a single master quality, it is better to see it as a complex metaphor of human worth with, in its narrative setting, at least three major (overlapping) referents—the "3 Rs" of response-ability, representation, and relationality. Each dimension has a range of human rights implications.

Response-ability

As creatures made in God's image, human beings *correspond* to God and are thus capable of being *responsible* to God. We correspond to God in the sense of being, like God, self-conscious, morally directed personalities capable of forming intimate, free and self-disclosing relationships, both with God and with one another. We are responsible both in the sense of having the capacity to respond to God (being "response-able") and of being accountable to God for this response and its consequences (being "responsible"). Both depend on the distinctively human attributes of reason, conscience, self-awareness, self-determination, and so on, but the image of God cannot be reduced to any one attribute. It refers to the responding person in his or her totality.

With respect to human rights, various *liberty rights*—such as freedom of conscience, freedom of speech and thought, freedom of religion—find their securest anchor in biblical anthropology. Arguably freedom is the master key to all human rights, for freedom, and respect for another's freedom, are prerequisites for entering into reciprocating relationships and exercising responsibility. In creating humankind in the divine image, God has shared with humanity God's own relational freedom in order that creative and imaginative relationship may exist between God and human beings.[70] God's radical respect for personal choice is shown in the freedom entrusted to Adam and Eve in the Garden.

The *right to life*, the most elementary human right, also finds its deepest justification here. Because humans are made in the image of God, who is the source of life, all possess inviolable sanctity. From its beginnings to its end, human life is a gift from God and should be respected as such (Ps. 139:13; 22:10; Jer. 1:5); God's image-bearers should not kill one another

(Gen. 9:6; Exod. 20:13).[71] God's words to Cain, "What have you done!," resonate with the inherent value of every human life (Gen. 4:10-11).

Because human life always exists in bodies, humans must also have the *right to security of person,* the right to remain whole, not to be abused or maimed or tortured or starved or molested.[72] The right to life includes the *right to the means of life* as well—food, shelter, clothing, and health.

Perhaps the most critical implication is the *primacy of responsibility* in the operation of human rights. It is not just that every right carries a corresponding duty not to infringe rights of others (a commonplace in secular theory). More profoundly, humans are responsible to God for others' welfare. Human obligation is not primarily to other persons but *to* God *for* other persons. "Where is your brother, Abel?" God asks Cain (Gen. 4:9). Such responsibility cannot be evaded; it is a constituent element of our humanness. Nor can such responsibility be discharged simply by non-interference with another's liberty. Being "my brother's keeper" includes practical concern for and positive action on behalf of other image-bearers.[73]

In view of this, human rights may be thought of as the rights each person has to have other persons fulfill their responsibility to God with regard to him or her. As Christopher Wright observes, "responsibility to God for others and rights under God in respect of others are inseparably correlative. Where one exists, the other cannot be denied."[74]

Representation

In the Genesis text, the divine image forms the basis for humankind's vocation to exercise limited dominion over the earth and to care for and cultivate creation, as God's representative. Just as a statue represents a god, human beings represent the Creator God. They are means by which God's rule is made visibly present in the world. In using the nouns *image* and *likeness* (which also occur in Mesopotamian royal inscriptions), the text depicts the first human in royal terms.

In Mesopotamian cosmogonies, human beings are invariably portrayed as slaves, created to maintain the universe for the gods and to feed them through temple sacrifice. When the accounts include a king, he is created separately as mediator between heaven and earth and has the role of overseeing the service offered by human beings to the gods. In the biblical tradition, however, humankind as a whole is appointed as God's royal vice-regent in the world (cf. Ps. 8:6). "The God of Genesis does not require human servants in the manner of other gods; the human race consequently has a different relation to work and to the world."[75]

The common jurisdiction humans are given over nonhuman creation carries a wide range of implications for *environmental, social and economic rights*, which I deal with later. It also relativizes all human political structures, and thus justifies those *civil and political rights* that protect persons from rulers who claim all significant authority for themselves. "Human beings do not exist for the sake of rule," says Jürgen Moltmann, "rule, rather, exists for the sake of human beings."[76]

Relationality

The fascinating shift from singular to plural forms in the sequence of the canonical creation accounts points to another crucial dimension of the divine image—it is possessed fully by every individual, but it is known, expressed, and fulfilled only in social relationships.

On the one hand, God creates an individual being in the divine image. Other creatures are created in multiplicities. In Genesis 1 God creates "waters" and "lights" and "plants" and "swarms of living creatures" (1:20), birds and animals and fish and so on. Then God creates "Adam" (1:26). The noun is singular and generic ("humankind"), and although it is indicated that Adam consists of many individuals ("let *them* have dominion," "male and female he created *them*"), their plurality derives from their generic unity as Adam. The singular nature of humankind is even more obvious in Genesis 2 where God creates only one earth creature in God's own image, to serve as the ancestor of all other human beings (cf. Gen. 5:3).

Two important deductions bearing on human rights can be made from this fact. One is that every individual bears the image of God in equal measure, a point not lost on the later rabbis.

The Rabbis, the classical commentators on the Torah, were intrigued about why that account is couched in terms of a single individual rather than in terms of multitudes. The story, they state, is cast in this way to teach the value of the worth of the individual. Every individual person is equivalent to that first human created by God. Thus, each person is of supreme value. Whoever harms a single person is as if they harmed all of God's creation. Whoever benefits a single person is as if they had benefited all creation. Indeed, each of us, equivalent to that first ancestor, is entitled to boast, "On account of me was the world created" and, conversely, required to bear on our shoulders the consequences of such responsibility.[77]

The other deduction is that because every human has a common ancestor, there is a basic equality beneath all human distinctions of race, class, rank, or religion. All people are cosmically children of the same Father (Mal. 2:10), common descendants of Adam, hence biologically kin to each other.

On the other hand, both creation accounts make it clear, in different ways, that humanity necessarily implies *co-humanity*. It is impossible to be human alone; relationality is intrinsic to human nature. It is intrinsic because it is of the nature of God to be in relationship, not only with creation but supremely within God's own self. From a Christian Trinitarian perspective, God's "personality" consists in being a communion of persons: "let *us* make humankind in *our* image." This intra-divine fellowship is the pattern for intra-human fellowship. Just as the Triune God exists in eternal, intimate, equalitarian relationship within the Godhead, so human beings are created to know intimate, enduring, equalitarian relationships with each other. "Only in human fellowship with other people is the human person truly an image of God (Gen. 1:28)."[78]

Such relationships take many forms, but it is the unique complementarity of male and female, with all its self-disclosing and life-giving potential, that most powerfully represents the divine image: "in the image of God he created him; male and female he created them" (Gen. 1:27; 5:1-2). Sexuality is thus a quality of the divine image, not in the sense that God is sexual but in the sense that God is the source of, and model for, self-disclosing, self-giving, intramural relationality.

Specific human rights deductions follow from this third dimension of the divine image. Most obvious is the *equal dignity and equal rights of male and female*. Neither gender possesses the divine image in isolation from the other. Thus when the dignity and rights of women are denied, the divine image in men is diminished.

Again, the relational nature of human existence suggests that rights are best conceived not as abstract qualities or "things" that inhere within autonomous individuals, but as *ingredients of relationships*. They therefore intersect with other relational qualities, such as loyalty, obligation, self-sacrifice, and love. To speak of individuals possessing inherent rights gives primacy to autonomy, privacy, individual agency, and personal choice. When viewed as relational attributes however, rights accent fraternity, interdependence, and responsibility.[79]

Relationality also underscores the validity of *collective or community rights*. The right to peaceful assembly, for example, is not simply a liberty right; it stems from the intrinsic sociality of human personhood. Social rights and duties are just as fundamental as individual rights and duties. Nurturing community, seeking the common good, and restoring broken relationships are as foundational to human rights as individual liberty.

Clearly, then, the importance of the biblical account of creation for human rights cannot be exaggerated.[80] It establishes the exceptional worth of every human being as a creature made in God's image, entrusted with responsibilities befitting such dignity and bearing rights that enable each person to remain true to his or her identity as God's image bearer. Having rights as a free creature made in God's image is, as Kieran Cronin puts it, "literally a 'status symbol' which one can hardly do without."[81]

The rights to liberty, life, and equality derive directly from this status, as does the right to participate in, and to be responsible for, various expressions of community. The inseparability of rights and responsibilities also finds unique grounding in the conception of human beings created to correspond to God and to represent God's rule over the earth.

FURTHER IMPLICATIONS FOR HUMAN RIGHTS

In addition to establishing the unique worth, social responsibilities, and fundamental equality of all human beings, five further implications of the creation story for human rights doctrine may be identified.

First, the origin of human rights in God's creative activity guarantees their *inalienability*. Since human rights derive from human dignity, which in turn derives from humankind's status as the *imago Dei*, the full panoply of human rights must be understood as gifts of God. Humanity has no autonomous "right" to such rights, for no one has the right to be created, much less created in God's image. They come gratuitously as the outworking of God-given dignity. Paradoxically, it is their gift-character that guarantees them as rights. If they were of human origin, humans could unmake them. As grants from a faithful God, their inalienability is secure.

Second, from a biblical perspective human rights can be nothing other than *universal* in scope. This is based not simply on the common attributes of human nature or the common interest of human communities, but on the existence and character of the one God who imparts his image equally to every human being. Since that image cannot be reduced to any master quality and is not linked to any secondary distinction of race, class, gender, nationality, or religion, there can be no grounds for excluding anyone from having human rights. As part of the creation order, human rights norms apply to all cultures, at all times, and no one is exempt from their authority.[82]

Third, the creation accounts underscore the *indivisibility* of human rights. Western countries stress the priority of first-generation rights; non-Western countries emphasise second- and third-generation rights. But because the divine image relates to the totality of the human experience of responsibility, representation, and relationality, and because of our inseparable unity as body and soul, there can be no normative justification for favoring individual rights over social, cultural, and economic rights, or vice versa. "Whatever violates the human dignity, whether the denial of due process of law or of sufficient food, violates human rights. Whatever is required for the protection of human dignity, whether freedom of worship or an adequate wage, must be recognized as a human right."[83] All human rights are indivisible and interdependent (Jan Lochman employs the Trinitarian notion of "perichoresis" or co-inherence to underline this point).[84]

Of course, the realities of human history and the constraints of circumstance require that priorities are set. In situations of political oppression, individual rights may need greater emphasis. In situations of economic exploitation and social injustice, social and economic rights may require more attention. But it is still important to acknowledge the principle of indivisibility so that where an enduring imbalance develops it may be challenged on the highest authority. For to honor a human being as the image of God requires us to acknowledge all human rights in the same degree and therefore to view them in their indissoluble relationship to each other.[85]

Fourth, the biblical accounts of creation suggest there is *an irreducibility in both individual and communal rights* which stands as a corrective both to socialist or tribal collectivism and to Western liberal individualism. The creation accounts show that individuality and communality are equal aspects of human personality, distinguishable but inseparable. This requires a dynamic interplay between the rights and duties of individuals and of groups. Both have irreducible validity.

Rights claims to private property and free commerce, for example, must never be used to legitimize unjust social structures or to undermine the integrity of the community. Nor should collective rights be used to justify the violation of individual dignity in the name of some corporate good. As Moltmann observes, "the rights of persons can only be developed in a just society, and a just society can only be developed on the ground of the rights of the person."[86]

Finally, the creation narratives offer the most powerful *motivation* imaginable for observing human rights and freedoms. Grounding human rights in the divine image constitutes them as sacred entitlements. They belong to God as well as humanity.[87] Their neglect is a sin against the Creator; their abuse is sacrilege, the desecration of something most holy, the violation of God in person. To oppress any other human being on the basis of secondary distinctions is to insult God. "The one

who oppresses the poor shows contempt for their Maker"
(Prov. 14:31). Conversely, the observance of human rights
brings glory and honor to God, for God imparts divine glory
to humankind with the imago Dei.[88]

In secular theory, human rights are sanctioned by human
agreement. In biblical thought they are anchored in an answerability *coram Deo*, "before God." This answerability extends to the special duties entrusted to human beings in the
so-called cultural mandate, which is the second "moment" of
the biblical narrative.

4

Cultural Mandate: Human Rights Activate in Stewardship

BEARING OF THE DIVINE IMAGE, we have seen, implies correspondence and representation. Humankind serves as God's representative on earth insofar as it corresponds to God's own person. Accordingly, when the account of the creation of human beings in Genesis 1 is followed by the call to exercise dominion over nonhuman creation (Gen. 1:26-28), the implication is that the form of human rule must correspond to God's own loving, faithful, and life-sustaining rule over creation. Human beings "image" God both by loving what God loves and by imitating, albeit it in a derivative and limited way, God's action of sustaining and enhancing the flourishing of other created beings.[89] Only then is humanity's creation in the image of God fulfilled.

The imago Dei is therefore both an indicative (a given conformity to God) and an imperative (a requirement to choose conformity to God's character and rule in fulfilling the cultural mandate). As Moltmann puts it, "the dignity of human beings consists in this, that they are human and should be human. Their existence is gift and task simultaneously."[90]

HUMAN RIGHTS IMPLICATIONS

The task entrusted to human beings and the responsibility to perform it in conformity to God's will together evoke a range of human rights implications. Most obvious, again, is the *inseparability of rights and responsibilities*. As Paul Marshall observes, "Human beings have the right to do what God calls them to do. Their rights relate to their God-given human duties and responsibilities. Human beings have a right to the institutions and resources they need to carry out their responsibilities."[91] Stewardship is what we are made for; we are responsible to live up to our calling; rights give us claim to what is necessary to fulfill this responsibility.

A less obvious implication but still legitimate is the *right to personal fulfillment*. Work, before the Fall, is a blessing, the primary means of people achieving self-realization. Christians are often uncomfortable with talk of self-fulfillment (or "the pursuit of happiness," as the American Declaration of Independence puts it) because it sounds egotistical and self-serving. But some such right is implied by the fact that God's image is both gift and potential. Human beings have the right to achieve the potential of their humanity, the right to be and to become fully human. The mode of self-actualization is not self-determined however, as in much contemporary thought. It occurs through living in conformity to God's will and God's way of exercising dominion over the earth.

From this issues a range of *environmental or ecological rights and duties*. Human beings possess dignity superior to that of the flora and fauna and have the right to use them for their own benefit (Gen. 1:29-30; cf. Matt. 7:26). But at the same time human beings are part of the created order, dependent on it for their own survival and responsible to God for its care. Plundering, exploitation, and destruction of nature are not simply unwise or shortsighted; rather, they fundamentally contradict human dignity and the "rights" of creation to be ruled in a God-like way. Human rule is only rightful when it is exercised "in cooperation and community with the environment and leads to life-giving symbiosis between human society and the natural environment."[92] From a biblical perspective, then, third- and fourth-generation rights are intrinsic to the human condition. (Even the personification of creation implied in ascribing "rights" to the environment can claim solid biblical precedent.)

So too are second generation rights, for various *social and economic rights* are implied by the cultural mandate. For example, all people are given dominion over the earth; all therefore have equal right of access to the earth's resources. Such stewardship entails property rights in terms of a right to control specific resources; hence the injunctions in biblical law against stealing and covetousness (Exod. 20:15; Deut. 5:21) and stipulations requiring restitution (Exod. 22:5-14). But the right to property is not, as often it is in Western practice, the right to exclusive, private possession for one's own benefit. Ultimate ownership remains with God (Ps. 24:1); the divine landlord gives *all* human beings right of access to his property (cf. Ps. 115:16) to enable them to fulfill their calling as God's stewards, to serve God and neighbor. Accordingly, as Wright puts it, "the right of all to *use* is before the right of any to *own*."[93]

Every person is called to engage in productive work to "fill the earth and subdue it." Everyone therefore has the *right to meaningful work*, as well as to *periodic rest from work* (Gen. 2:3). This means not only that individuals are responsible to work themselves (cf. 2 Thess. 3:6-13) but also to enable or allow others to work. Indeed, "to prevent another person working, or to deny or deprive him of work, is to offend against his humanity and the image of God in him, as well as failing in one's responsibility to God for him."[94] The right to work includes the *right to the necessities of work,* such as education and training, the means of production, a living wage, participation in trade and exchange, and a voice in decision-making.

Insofar as such rights stem from the mandate given commonly to all humanity, they are necessarily conditioned by justice. Uncontrolled economic growth at the expense of the environment is a denial of ecological justice. Unbalanced economic growth in which some live in luxury and entirely control the means of production while others lack food, shelter or clothing is a denial of economic justice. Both are a desecration of God's image.

THE ENTRY OF SIN

In biblical perspective, environmental destruction, economic exploitation and social injustice are the result of God's image-bearers falling into sin—that is, choosing *not* to conform themselves to God's will and lordship. Contrary to what some think, the Fall does not destroy or attenuate human rights (with sinners forfeiting all rights before God). Nor is it the occasion for the initial giving of rights (to afford sinners protection from other sinners).[95] Rights are given in the structures of creation, not in reply to the Fall, even if the need of them is intensified, and their misuse and abuse multiplied, because of the Fall. Rights are the flipside of human responsibility to God, and if responsibility remains after the Fall, so do rights.[96] Even Cain, the convicted murderer, enjoys certain rights inasmuch as God holds others responsible for how they treat him (Gen. 4:15).

But the entry of sin does have several consequences for human rights. The divine image is marred, though not erased. Humankind's knowledge of God is corrupted (cf. Rom. 1:18-23), limiting its potential for conformity to God's will. Humanity's relationship with the earth also becomes dysfunctional. The environment now resists human habitation (Gen. 3:18) and work becomes toil and hardship (Gen. 3:17,19), with the potential to enslave as well as fulfill human beings. Human dominion over creation becomes exploitative and destructive.[97] Relationships within the human family are also poisoned, with people failing to acknowledge the equal dignity of other human beings, exemplified by Cain's murder of Abel (Gen. 4:1-16).

This first murder, indeed, is the first recorded failure in the biblical story to respect a human right.[98] Desiring to go its own way, humankind scorned human life, then trampled human rights on a massive scale (Gen. 4:23-24), so that "the earth was corrupt in God's sight and the earth was filled with violence" (6:11).

It is this sinful and distorted empirical reality that now becomes the occasion for God's redemptive activity to renew God's image in humanity, initially through the agency of a covenant people under covenant law, a law which, amongst other things, positivizes human rights.

5

Covenant: Human Rights Are Expressed in Covenant Law

Of central importance in the biblical narrative is the theme of *covenant*. A covenant is a formal agreement or treaty between two parties which establishes a committed and enduring relationship. When two parties enter a covenant, a new moral community is formed, based on a common recognition of the worth and dignity of the other and generating a range of mutual rights and obligations which both must honor. The driving force that advances and unifies the biblical story are the covenant relationships that God enters into with human beings and human communities.

There are different kinds of covenant in the Bible. It is common to distinguish, for example, between *conditional* (or law) covenants and *unconditional* (or promissory) covenants. God's covenants with Noah (Gen. 9:8-17), Abraham (Gen. 15; 17), and David (2 Sam. 7) are examples of promissory covenants, in which God issues a solemn commitment without specifying reciprocal obligations. The Sinai covenant (Exod. 20) is a law covenant. Here God initiates the relationship with Israel but specifies obedience to the law as the condition for maintenance of the relationship. In principle, Israel's failure to meet her obligations releases God from commitment to Israel.

This distinction must not be pressed too far, however. Even in promissory covenants, human obligations, sometimes of a very radical type, are implied. Indeed, as Kieran Cronin notes, "covenant relationship initiated by God which does not impose the obligation of a moral response is not worthy of God and only undermines human dignity."[99]

A more helpful distinction for our purposes is between *inclusive* covenants, which embrace the whole human race, and *special* covenants formed with limited groups within humanity to advance God's purposes for the race at large. God's special covenant with Israel explicitly and repeatedly bars the entry of any third party, be it another deity or another people, but it was still intended to bring a blessing on the third party of the human race. It was a means to an end—God's goal of redeeming all those within the inclusive covenant (cf. Gen. 22:18).

SPECIAL RIGHTS AND HUMAN RIGHTS

We saw in chapter 2 that the inclusive covenant formed between God and human beings in creation (cf. Hos. 6:7), and reaffirmed in the covenant with Noah (Gen. 9:8), gives rise to a range of universal human rights. In this chapter we will see how God's special covenant with Israel also generates rights, many codified in biblical law and tradition. Some writers happily describe these laws as human rights.[100] Others hesitate to do so, partly because several items of the law fall below modern human rights' standards and partly because they lack the crucial qualification of universality: the law was intended for Israel alone, not for the entire human race.[101]

Perhaps the best strategy is to view the provisions of Mosaic law not as human rights *per se* but as "special rights" deriving from the special covenant. But there remains a crucial connection between both kinds of rights.[102] Special rights are a particular application of human rights. On the one hand, they give institutional expression to fundamental human rights principles within the constraints of contingent and sinful historical contexts. On the other hand, they equip the covenant community to be "a light to the nations" (Isa. 42:6; 49:3,6; cf. Exod. 19:5-6). They enable that community to serve as God's primary instrument for achieving the larger goal of the inclusive covenant—the bringing of the human race into its full rights as children of God (cf. John 1:12). "In the biblical drama," as Herbert Brichto puts it, "the rest of mankind waits in the wings as Israel holds center stage. It is Israel's career now which will determine whether mankind can have a model for success, or whether man will fail in this particular prototype as he previously had in the universal history."[103]

There is thus a crucial universalism within Judeo-Christian tradition, obscured sometimes by the elect people's ethnocentrism and religious exclusivism (both Jewish and Christian), but still basic to its identity and task.[104] It is not a universalism, of course, in the modern sense of all religious and moral perspectives being deemed equally valid. It is a universalism in the sense that the particular vocation of the covenant community is considered to be for the universal benefit of all people.

This imposes limits on Israel's rights. Although she concedes the right of foreign peoples to worship other gods,[105] and acknowledges her own freedom to do so should she choose (Josh. 24:15), Israel claims no "human right" to religious liberty for herself. She has been elected by the one true God (Deut. 6:4), and her special rights are restricted by God's "right" to her loyalty.

Now this approach of recognizing the distinction yet connection between special rights (in covenant law) and human rights (in creation) enables us to affirm the human rights ideals present in biblical law and at the same time acknowledge the contingency or imperfection of their concrete expression in positive legislation and societal institutions. These laws and institutions, as noted earlier, are best viewed paradigmatically rather than prototypically or legalistically. This means they provide us with models of how essential human rights values and principles found social expression in the ancient world, but we are not bound to replicate the models in detail.[106]

Nor, incidentally, are we bound to exaggerate the uniqueness of Israelite law, as if it fell ready-made from heaven. There are several unique features to Old Testament law, but a considerable amount of it appears to be a restatement of customary law and folk tradition already ancient and widespread throughout Mesopotamia. The revelatory nature of biblical law consists not in the fact that God proclaims previously unknown ethical norms, but in the way God's own name and character are placed behind certain familiar norms. Put simply, it is not so much that God reveals the law as the law reveals God.

This is why the biblical writers sometimes treat God's law as Israel's unique possession, and sometimes regard it as but the inscripturation of a universal law to which all nations are accountable and, to some degree, can know (Amos 1:3-2:3; cf. Rom. 1:18-2:29). This is another reason why it is legitimate to see a connection between special rights and human rights.[107]

HUMAN RIGHTS IN BIBLICAL LEGISLATION

Biblical law is a vast and complex system of provisions and prohibitions. Thus all we can hope to do here is provide examples of how recognition of human dignity and human rights informs if not permeates the system.

Contrary to what some say, the language of "rights" is not completely absent in Old Testament law and its application. James Barr points to "certain departments within the manifold meanings of that many-sided word *mishpat*" which seem to attach rights to the family, position, class, or function of persons.[108] Deuteronomy 21:17 affirms an inalienable right to the status and privileges of being a firstborn son. This cannot be taken away even if the father wishes to transfer it to another son of a different marriage. Jeremiah 32:7-8 speaks of rights of inheritance and of redemption belonging to family members, while Deuteronomy 18:3 speaks of the rights of priests to receive certain portions of the sacrifices.

More significant are texts which speak to rights of widows, orphans, the poor, and resident foreigners (e.g., Exod. 23:6; Deut. 24:17). This comes closer to the notion of rights that attach to a person in virtue of being human, since any person could potentially become a widow, an orphan, a poor person. Should they do so, certain rights came into play.[109]

Two other Hebrew words sometimes evoke the sense of rights. The word *dîn* comes from the root meaning to "act as a judge, advocate, or ruler," and can refer to the place of judgment, the cause of action and the action itself. Where it denotes the cause of action, it comes close to our concept of rights. Thus in Proverbs 31:8 the king is urged to advocate the "rights" (NRSV) of the destitute, and Jeremiah criticizes his people for failing to plead the rights of the fatherless in such a way as to succeed (Jer. 5:28). The key words *sedeq/sedeqah* are usually translated as righteousness or justice.[110] At its most basic level, righteousness refers to behavior consistent with the demands of a relationship, including the idea of honoring the claims of the other party. Isaiah 5:23 uses the term to speak of the claims or rights of the innocent to acquittal.

Taken together, *mishpat* and *sedeqah* (especially as a hendiadys)[111] convey much of the Bible's teaching on social justice. Given that "the concept of justice . . . permeates all human rights,"[112] these terms are obviously relevant to our inquiry. But only rarely is either used specifically for the holding of rights.

Of course the concept of rights may still operate behind passages where no normative word for rights is used and even where the mode of expression seems antithetical to rights. A case in point is the Ten Commandments (Exod. 20; Deut. 5). At first glance there seems little connection with human rights. Rather than affirming rights, the Decalogue imposes duties; instead of proclaiming freedoms, it contains only prescriptions and prohibitions. But appearances can be deceptive. One Old Testament scholar has described the Decalogue as Israel's "Bill of Rights,"[113] while one architect of the Universal Declaration of Human Rights has termed the UDHR "a worthy extension" of the Ten Commandments.[114]

The reason for this linking of the Decalogue with human rights lies in the *function* it serves. The Ten Commandments are the foundational charter of a people recently liberated from servitude in Egypt (with all its human rights abuses) and now constituted as an independent nation able to enjoy her rights of freedom. To preserve this freedom, Israel's rights are expressed in the characteristic biblical idiom of responsibilities.

These responsibilities constitute a *response* to what God has done and entail *conformity* to the will and character of God

("I am the Lord your God who brought you out of Egypt, therefore you must . . . "). Their right and freedom to worship God has been achieved through the exodus; a range of responsibilities now follow:

- They now have the responsibility to worship God exclusively (No. 1).
- They must not render God as a lifeless image or idol (No. 2), which would enslave them afresh.
- They have seen the meaning of God's name demonstrated in liberation; they have the responsibility not to use that name selfishly, maliciously or foolishly (No. 3).
- They have been freed from the indignity of slavery; now they have the responsibility to preserve the right of regular Sabbath rest for themselves, and even for their animals (No. 4).
- Freed from Pharaoh's violence against their family life, they now must protect the family by respecting its parental authority (No. 5) and sexual integrity (No. 7).
- Delivered from infanticide and terror, they must respect human life and not tolerate murder (No. 6).
- No longer aliens in a foreign land but possessors of a their own land, they must not steal or covet what is God's gift to all (Nos. 8, 10).
- Aware of God's justice, they must not betray one another by perverted testimony (No. 9).

Understood thus, the Decalogue gives voice to basic human rights convictions.[115]

KEY HUMAN RIGHTS CONVICTIONS

The remainder of Old Testament social and religious law can be seen as the detailed application of the central principles or rights affirmed in the Ten Commandments. "One could go through Old Testament laws and institutions," Christopher Wright maintains, "and compile a fascinating pattern of human rights, inferring them from the kaleidoscopic range of human responsibility embodied in them."[116] Here it will be enough to illustrate how four fundamental human rights convictions (life, equality, freedom, and solidarity) can be discerned within covenant law and practice.

The right to life

We have seen how the creation of human beings in God's image implies a right to life, which must be understood as a sacred gift of God. The sanctity of human life strongly informs biblical law. In the Hebrew penal code, for example, life is valued more highly than property. Cuneiform law sometimes rates financial loss as more serious than loss of life. In biblical law no property offense, in normal legal procedure, carried the death penalty, while theft of a person for gain (kidnapping) did (Exod. 21:16; Deut. 24:7). Premeditated murder was also a capital offense, based on the talionic "life for a life" principle (Exod. 21:23-25; 21:12; Lev. 24:21; Deut. 19:19-21). Deliberate murder, moreover, is unique among the capital offenses in Old Testament law in that no ransom or substitute penalty is permitted, preventing the wealthy from escaping the consequences of despising the life of their social inferiors (Num. 35:31; Deut. 19:13).

In specifying a life for a life, the *lex talionis* combines a reverence for human life (as bearer of God's image, cf. Gen. 9:6) with a strict limitation on the extinguishing of human life. Death cannot be exacted in repayment for lesser crimes than murder, like wounds or insults or dishonor or theft (cf. Gen. 4:23). The penalty furthermore must fall on the murderer alone; no sanction is given for blood feuds against the perpetrator's family or clan.[117]

Biblical law also seeks to protect human life from accidental death or negligence. For example, builders must make parapets for roofs of houses to prevent people falling to their death (Deut. 22:8). Owners of a dangerous ox must be warned to keep it in lest it gore and kill a person (Exod. 21:29). So valuable is human life that even animals must pay the penalty for involvement in shedding innocent blood (cf. Gen. 9:5), a detail unique to Israelite law. Even in capital offenses, stringent safeguards emerged in Pentateuchal law to prevent the accidental or deliberate miscarriage of justice.[118] Meanwhile the distinction between murder and manslaughter (Num. 35:10-29) and the creation of cities and other places of refuge (Num. 35; Deut. 4:19; Josh. 20; 1 Chron. 6:67) also functioned to preserve life.

The dignity of human life is reflected in other features of penal practice as well. As Wright observes, "there is a humanitarian ethos in Israelite penal law which is acknowledged by all who have compared it with ancient Near Eastern collections of law."[119] Criminals are regarded as human persons with rights protected by God. For example, Deuteronomy 25:2-3 sets a limit to corporal punishment so that the offender is "not degraded in your sight."[120]

Unlike all ancient Near Eastern codes, physical mutilation is all but absent as a judicial penalty (except for the extreme, unlikely, and bizarre situation envisaged in Deut. 25:11-12). No form of imprisonment is prescribed in the law, although it was a feature of later monarchic practice.

Even the punishment of enslavement for some offenses was probably more humane than is modern imprisonment. At least the slave was still free to enjoy marital and family life, and he or she remained part of the community, participated in its festivals and seasons, and did meaningful work with the rest of the community—things which imprisonment denies.[121]

Earlier we saw that the right to life includes the right to the means of life. There is little reflection in the Hebrew Bible on what comprises the means of life, but Douglas Knight suspects it entailed more than the bare necessities for sheer survival. Vital needs are not only those that ensure the animation of the body but all that is necessary for human enhancement. Evident here is

> an understandable notion that, to be fully alive, an individual needs sustenance, health, and emotional stability. Anything short of these would be enervating and devitalizing. So viewed, the nature of human life carried with it moral claims on those elements which contributed to well-being. For anyone to deprive others of the basics necessary for a happy existence constituted immoral conduct. When the cause for distress seemed to lie outside human control, complaint could be brought against God. Life in this world was too precious to relinquish and too promising to accept anything less than ideal.[122]

Covenant law, then, seems conditioned by an appreciation of the right to life—and to a certain quality of life, which humans enjoy as creatures in God's image. It must be said, however, that this appreciation is not identical with that reflected in secular human rights theory. It is not an absolute right to life that inheres in autonomous individuals. Limited by the nature of covenant membership and associated religious understandings, it may be set aside in certain circumstances.[123]

Around twenty offenses carry the death penalty in Mosaic law, including such things as adultery, incest, blasphemy, and Sabbath-breaking.[124] Here capital punishment serves to protect the integrity of the covenant community, which was thought to suffer ritual pollution from certain serious sins. Execution of the offender was a cultic or religious requirement for "cleansing the land" of evil and safeguarding the holiness of the people of God (Num. 35:33).

As Moshe Greenberg explains, "Capital crimes are a blot on the whole community. When the law decrees that the capital offender must die, it is not merely to punish him but to "purge the evil from Israel" (Deut. 17:12; cf. 13:5-11; 13:16; 17:7; 19:19; 21:21; 22:21-22, 24; 24:7; Judg. 20:13; 2 Sam. 19:13)."[125] The infliction of death, in other words, functioned as a ritual expiation or act of atonement for sin (hence the close parallel that exists between the scapegoat and sin-offering rituals in Lev. 4:15; 16:21, and the ritual associated with the execution of blasphemers in Lev. 24:14).

By contemporary standards, such treatment of criminals might suggest a cavalier attitude to human life. Within an Israelite covenantal framework, however, it suggests that the right to life was communal as well as individual. "Their readiness to eliminate certain criminals and enemies arose out of a desire to eradicate what was held to be severe threats to the very existence of all other Israelites. . . . The imperative to live was not to be subverted by any others, whether from within or without, who might take the life of Israelites."[126] It also shows how seriously commitment to the common good was expected of individual covenant members.

Equality

As slaves in Egypt, the Israelites were at the bottom of a rigidly hierarchical and oppressive social order. But God intervened to liberate them and to constitute them as an independent, covenanted society, a society in which the memory of former servitude would be deliberately kept alive to prevent, or critique the emergence of, oppressive structures. "In this way," Richard Bauckham explains, "the exodus was the source of a radically egalitarian ideal, frequently forgotten but always there to be recovered and applied in criticism of hierarchy and privilege."[127]

God's covenant relationship with Israel was with the whole people, not just her elites, and it entailed an equality of covenant standing across age, sex and rank.

> You stand assembled today, all of you, before the Lord your God—the leaders of your tribes, your elders, and your officials, all the men of Israel, your children, your women, and the aliens who are in your camp, both those who cut your wood and those who draw your water—to enter into the covenant of the Lord your God, sworn by an oath, which the Lord your God is making with you today. (Deut. 29:10-12)

Accordingly the "rights" of covenant membership applied to all. The right to rest, for example, applied to "you, your son or your daughter, your male or female slave, your livestock, or the alien resident in your towns" (Exod. 20:9). Among other things, the Sabbath provision demonstrated that the object of human life is not to maximize productivity but to manage, develop, and enjoy God's good creation as God's image-bearers.

Of course, social and economic inequalities did exist within the covenant community, and more so after the advent of monarchy.[128] But covenant law included several egalitarian features which are "the staples of contemporary human rights law"—due process, fairness in criminal procedures, equity in civil law.[129] Judges are not to accept bribes (Deut. 16:19) but are required to be impartial to homeborn and stranger alike (Lev. 24:22; Deut. 27:19), to the needy and to the powerful (Lev. 19:15), to the rich and the poor (Deut. 1:16-17; Exod. 23:2-3,6). The right to a fair trial (Deut. 19:15) and to fair punishment (Exod. 21:23-25) are also required equally for all. Even slaves enjoyed certain legal protections (e.g., Exod. 21:20-21; Deut. 23:15-16). Those most vulnerable to injustice in a patriarchal society—widows and orphans and sojourners—are singled out for special care. The king is charged with protecting especially the rights of such people (Ps. 72:2,4). King and commoner were equally subject to covenantal law. The divine king, not the human king, was considered to own the land. The king's powers were therefore expressly limited, in a way that would prevent tyranny. The king was to have no independent powerbase centered on private wealth, nor a standing army or foreign alliances (Deut. 17:14-20; cf.1 Sam. 8:11-18). Royal decrees contrary to the demands of divine law were not considered binding (Exod. 1:15-17; 1 Kings 21). Kings could not abrogate the rights of their subjects without protest, especially from the prophets (e.g., 2 Sam. 12:1-15; Jer. 22:13-17). For Louis Henkin, all this constitutes a type of "limited 'constitutional' government, the jurisprudential ancestor of contemporary human rights."[130]

None of this is to say that Israel fully embodied the ideal of equality implied in the creation narratives. The inferior position assigned to those who were not free adult males (women, children, slaves, foreigners) falls short of the principle of human equality given in creation. Yet in another sense, the ideal was still operative inasmuch as the inferior status of such groups is never explicitly based on the assumption that they are less alive, less human, or of less inherent value, or that their nature is essentially different. It is a functional inferiority due to historical and sociological conditions, not an ontological or normative condition.[131]

Viewed in a similar way are those supplanted, sometimes brutally exterminated, during the conquest of Canaan. They are not regarded as subhuman or less human than the chosen people. They are said to have forfeited their right to territory due to a long history of sin, including such "crimes against humanity" as infant sacrifice (Gen. 15:14,16; Deut. 9:4-6). In addition, God warns Israel against encroaching on the rights of neighboring peoples who in earlier times had also, under divine sovereignty, supplanted sinful inhabitants (Deut. 2:4-5, 9-12, 19-23).

A similar thing can be said with respect to the Hebrew institution of slavery. Slavery is not considered a "natural" condition (Job 31:15) and is never condoned as an enduring state, except where freely chosen. Social and economic inequality, in other words, did not imply a lesser humanity or a lack of human dignity.

Freedom

No value (or right) was more precious to Israel than freedom. The reason for this is obvious: she owed her existence as a nation to God's intervention to liberate her from slavery in Egypt. Israel's collective memory of her time of enslavement and of God's act of deliverance was one of the most powerful factors in shaping Israel's social laws and institutions in a humanitarian direction. The covenant charter itself is predicated on God's gift of freedom ("I am the Lord your God, who brought you out of the land of Egypt, out of the house of slavery," Exod. 20:2; Deut. 5:6). Meanwhile the repeated admonition to remember that "You were once slaves in Egypt" is invoked in the Torah as "the warrant for all acts of social righteousness," including the rights to a fair judicial process.[132]

Even the Sabbath institution (with both weekly and annual forms), which conferred rights of rest on all within Israel's borders, including slaves, is explained in Deuteronomy by the experience of enslavement and liberation (Deut. 5:15). Free people can rest; slaves cannot—except in Israel!

This points to something deeply paradoxical in Israel's conception of freedom. It is paradoxical in that although she was a nation of freed slaves, which constantly recalled the bitterness of slavery and the joys of liberation, Israel herself—like every other nation in antiquity—practiced slavery. Slaves in Israel were both foreigners captured as prisoners of war (Num. 31:9-12; Deut. 21:10-14; Judg. 1:28; 5:30; 1 Sam. 17:9; 2 Chron. 28:8) or bought for service (Lev. 25:44-45; cf. Gen. 37:28; Ezek. 27:13). And Israelites who had fallen disastrously into debt and had sold themselves into indentured service (Exod. 21:7; Deut. 15:12; Lev. 25: 39; Isa. 50:1).

But Israel's recollection of Egypt made her deeply uncomfortable with the institution.[133] In one sense she viewed the enslavement of free Israelites as an affront to the honor of Yahweh who had redeemed her from Egyptian servitude (Lev.

25:35-42; Deut. 15:12-15). Enslavement was not employed as a criminal punishment (cf. Exod. 22:1-3) and kidnapping for slavery was deemed an offense worthy of death (Exod. 21:16; Deut. 24:7).

Torah legislation, furthermore, served to mitigate some of slavery's more oppressive features, so much so that some question whether "slavery" is an appropriate term for the Hebrew practice of debt-bondage, since it evokes the very different reality of slavery in the European and American traditions.[134] Certainly the compiler of Leviticus 25 sees an important technical distinction between slavery involving foreigners and temporary debt-service rendered by fellow Hebrews, who should be treated no more harshly than hired workers. How this distinction squares with stipulations in the other biblical slave-codes (Exod. 21:2-11; Deut. 15:12-18),[135] or was reflected actual practice (1 Sam. 22:1-2; 2 Kings 4:1; Neh. 5:1-13; Prov. 22:7), is unclear. In any event, even debt-slavery was a practice open to serious abuse by the wealthy, as the prophets recognized (Jer. 34:13-16; Amos 2:6-7; 8:4-6). At times it threatened the fabric of Israelite society.[136]

What is most significant is that although slaves were subject to personal and economic liabilities, and legally were the property of the slave-owner whose interests took precedence over the slave's kinship obligations, slaves were still regarded as human beings, with God-given dignity and rights (cf. Job 31:13-15). Chief among these was the right to eventual freedom, without payment, after six years service (Exod. 21:2; Deut. 15:12) or in the year of Jubilee (Lev. 25:40), and with enough provisions to enable them to start a new life (Deut. 15:13-18). Manumission could also be bought, either by a kinsman-redeemer (Exod. 21:8; Lev. 25:48-49) or, "if they prosper, they may redeem themselves" (Lev. 25:49).

Upon release, slaves took their place as free members of the family, entitled to all attendant privileges and subject to no disadvantages. Unlike other Semitic societies, Israel appears to have had no class of "freed persons" of intermediate status between slaves and citizens. Only by voluntary, and painful, choice could a slave remain in the master's service permanently (Exod. 21:5-6; Deut. 15:16-17). Slaves were also entitled to Sabbath rest (Exod. 23:12) and, if circumcised, could participate in religious meals (Exod. 12:44; Deut. 12:12ff; 16:11-12; cf. Lev. 22:11). If taken as a wife, a female slave had rights to food, clothing, and conjugal relations (Exod. 21:10-11).

Slaves also enjoyed legal protection from severe physical mistreatment. A master who killed his slave would be prosecuted and punished; a master who knocked out the tooth or eye of a slave had to set the slave free with compensation (Exod. 21:20-21; cf. Deut. 21:10-14). Particularly impressive are the rights of asylum that applied to runaway slaves. In the ancient world, it was taken for granted that there was an obligation to return slaves to their masters. But Israelites are commanded to harbor runaway slaves (Deut. 23:15-16). Such a law, if effective, would have helped reduce the abuse of slaves, since harsh masters would not have been able to keep slaves.[137]

Built into Israel's practice of slavery, then, were limitations and freedoms which challenged the normative foundations of the institution, the logical outworking of which signaled eventual abolition of the practice. As Richard Bauckham comments,

> All relationships of subjection which permit the exploitation of one human being by another are contrary to the fundamental will of God as the Old Testament reveals it. They have no basis in the created status of human beings, who are all equally subject to God, and the historical purpose of God is for the abolition of all such relationships. His liberation of Israel from slavery cannot, in the end, be an exclusive privilege for Israel alone, but is prototypical of his will that all humanity should similarly come under his liberating lordship.[138]

Israel's conception of freedom was paradoxical in another way. It was a freedom experienced in subjection, a subjection to the totalitarian demands of her God. She was not free to do entirely as she pleased; she was bound to obey God's law. But because she believed that the most profound aspects of human identity are conferred upon human beings by the God who made them in his image, living in conformity with this God's will must be the highest form of freedom. As Max Stackhouse notes, "When the first Hebrew bowed his head to an ethical

God, beyond his own or any other culture, freedom was born. Freedom is a real possibility because there is a God; because there is a God there is a basis for real freedom."[139]

Participation

In the biblical tradition, as already observed, the rights of three groups in particular are often singled out for special mention. These are widows, orphans, and the poor (e.g., Isa. 10:1-2), sometimes together with sojourners or immigrants (Exod. 22:21-22; Deut. 24:19-22).[140] What these groups had in common in a patriarchal order was their vulnerability to exploitation. The widow has no husband to watch over her rights, the orphan has no parents, the poor person has no money, and the stranger has no friends or family. It is therefore doubly important that their rights be guarded. Such persons possess rights in virtue of their essential humanity. "The rich and the poor have this in common: the Lord is their Maker" (Prov. 22:2; cf. 14:31). But their rights are easily trampled on, and so they are in need special protection.

The one who affords such protection is none other than God in person. It is God who "maintains the rights of the poor" (Ps. 140:12). It is God who actively secures justice for the oppressed. It is God who declares, "You shall not abuse any widow or orphan. If you do abuse them. . . . I will kill you with the sword" (Exod. 22:21-23)!

God defends the weak in the first instance by including definite "welfare rights" in covenant law.[141] All the major legal collections of the Old Testament include protections for the poor.[142] By contrast, it is difficult to find a single clause that specifically protects the rights of the wealthy and powerful. Several laws guarantee right of access to food, even for the impoverished and landless (Deut. 14:28-29; 23:19-22, 24-25; Lev. 19:9-10; Exod. 23:10-11). Laws forbidding the expropriation of a debtor's cloak or livelihood imply a right to clothing and shelter (Exod. 22:26-27, Deut. 24:6, 12-13, 16-17; cf. Ezek. 18:5-7). Stipulations about prompt and fair payment for labor done imply a right to work and to fair wages (Lev. 19:13; cf. Deut. 24:15; Lev. 25:50-53), while laws requiring the well-off to provide interest-free loans to the poor presuppose their right to continued participation in productive activity (Deut. 23:19; 15:7-8).[143] Sabbath laws gave rights to rest and recreation equally across the social spectrum. If fully observed, Sabbatical and Jubilee regulations (Exod. 23:10-11; Deut. 15:1-11; Lev. 25:8-17, 23-55) would have also functioned to prevent the institutionalizing and absolutizing of poverty. Every seven years economic inequalities between creditors and debtors were to be righted and the land left fallow. Every forty-ninth or fiftieth year, slaves were to be released, debts remitted, and land restored to its owners, ensuring that the family could not be permanently dispossessed of land it had inherited equitably in the first place (Num. 33:54; Lev. 25:14-18, 25-34).

The utopian nature of the Jubilee regulations, together with the enormous practical difficulties entailed in putting them into practice,[144] has led to a general scholarly suspicion that the institution was never actually implemented. Firm evidence that it was practiced is very limited (cf. Neh. 5:1-13).[145] It is possible the Jubilee was not intended primarily to function as a realistic socioeconomic policy but as an ideal (or perhaps eschatological) benchmark against which to measure empirical practice. Certainly it came to serve this function, among others, in later Jewish and Christian history (cf. Isa. 61:1-2; Luke 4:18-19; Matt. 6:12; Acts 2:42-47; 4:32-35; 2 Cor. 6:2).[146]

But even in this capacity, what is most significant for us is that Jubilee regulations presuppose a right to participation in social and economic life by even the most marginal groups in society. These regulations also recognize the need for regular political action to restore such participatory rights, given the inherent tendency of all economic systems to concentrate wealth and power among the few at the expense of the many.

The cancellation of debts and return of forfeited land was known elsewhere in the ancient Near East. But the practice was usually limited to the king's retainers and was random in its occurrence. By contrast the biblical Jubilee was to be democratic in its effects and routine in its observance.[147] "The Jubilee legislation requires society to recognize a basic right of entitlement as part of being human," observes Hans Ucko. "The Jubilee is about freedom from the yoke of exploitation, a time of freedom for the enslaved and restoration of human dignity."[148] It also about care for the environment, for in guarding against the enduring exploitation of the poor, Jubilee regulations simultaneously guarded against over-exploitation of the land.

Such care for the impoverished and weak in biblical law is frequently mandated in the name of "justice and righteousness," not simply out of pity or charity or the quest for personal honor. The poor have a *right* to the basic ingredients of human existence—food, clothing, shelter, work, and rest—because in the abundance of creation the righteous God has supplied enough resources for everyone (Ps. 146.7). Extreme disparities must therefore be due to human injustice and require "righting" in the name of God's rightness or righteousness.

However, the primary and repeated reason Israelites are to care for the poor and the vulnerable is because this is the way God acted toward Israel in rescuing her from Egypt. "Remember that you were a slave in Egypt and the Lord your God redeemed you from there; *therefore* I command you to do this" (Deut. 24:18; cf. Exod. 22:21, emph. added). It is the particular responsibility of the king, the *most* powerful in the land, to imitate God's solidarity with oppressed people by championing the rights of the *least* powerful in the land, by protecting them from evildoers and intervening to remitting their debts.[149]

Another way in which God "pleads the cause of the poor" (Ps. 146:7) is by confronting the rich and the powerful with the challenge to do righteousness and justice with respect to the disadvantaged. When Israel forgets the covenant, it is the prophets, most explicitly Amos, Isaiah, and Jeremiah, who insist that fidelity to the covenant means honoring the rights of the poor and oppressed. "The prophets' portrayal of Israel's social injustice," notes Bruce Malchow, "is overwhelming."[150]

Among the things the prophets denounce are selfish hoarding of foodstuffs (cf. Num. 11:31-33) and the accumulation of surplus land and wealth (cf. Lev. 25:8-17), both of which are contrary to the welfare of the poor. If wealthy landowners or the religious establishment persist in trampling the rights of the poor, the prophets warn, God will come in judgment. "Ah you who make iniquitous decrees," Isaiah thunders, who write oppressive statutes, to turn aside the needy from justice and to rob the poor of my people of their right [*mishpat*], that widows may be your spoil, and that you may make the orphans your prey! What will you do on the day of punishment, in the calamity that will come from far away? (Isa. 10:1-3)

To become a faithful and just people again, Israel is summoned to true knowledge and true worship of God. This involves "not simply the recognition that another person has equal rights to the goods of God's creation" but also that the person is actively "securing these goods for them"[151] For from a biblical perspective, it is respect for the rights of the poor and defenseless which measures the health of the nation.

One final comment: the definite bias biblical teaching exhibits toward the poor and disadvantaged confirms rather than contradicts the principle of equality. In biblical terms, equality is not a matter of treating all people the same but compensating for given inequalities which prevent common participation in the life and benefits of the community. When God stands with the poor and downtrodden, it prevents the wealthy and powerful from seeing their abundance as a sign of God's favor. When God sides with the victims of injustice, God evens the balance with those who have the machinery of justice at their disposal and who can manipulate it for their own ends.

RIGHTS AND COMMUNITY

Enough has been said to demonstrate that covenant law declares, codifies, embodies, and nurtures key human rights values. Equally important is the fact that these values find expression within covenant community, within the context of human solidarity. In the biblical tradition, human rights are not simply the claims of isolated individuals against the state or against each another; they are the rights of people in community, bound together not simply by a social contract but by a sacred bond sustained by a shared memory of God's deliverance from slavery and a shared hope for the redemption of the world.[152] In this setting, rights do not exist to enable people to pursue their private interests but to build community—

a community that conforms to the love, justice and mercy of God. "Morality in Israel was heavily oriented toward relationships among persons," Knight points out, "indeed toward the creation of a moral society in which all persons would act in a manner conducive to the well-being of others."[153]

The next "moment" of the biblical story focuses on the life and ministry of a single individual, Jesus of Nazareth, who devoted his teaching and dedicated his life to the well-being of others. In New Testament interpretation, Jesus is presented not only as a sinless individual who lived a perfect human life before God (2 Cor. 5:21; Heb 4:15; 7:26-27; cf. John 8:21). He is also understood as one who embodies, as the Christ, Israel's Messiah, the destiny and hopes of the whole covenant community. More profoundly still, he is seen as one who represents the entire human race and, as the "last Adam" (1 Cor. 15:42-50; Rom. 5:12-21), restores humanity to its God-intended role in creation.

6

Christ: Human Rights are Sanctified by the Incarnation

T HE NEW TESTAMENT DOES NOT SPEAK directly of "human rights and freedoms" any more than does the Old Testament. The Greek noun *exousia* may be used in the sense of possessing a right or an authority to act, but the only one who possesses absolute exousia is God (Rom. 9:21; Matt. 20:15). God has shared divine exousia with the Son (Matt. 28:18), who therefore has the right on earth to forgive sins, to execute judgment and to give life (Mark 2:11; John 5:20-27).

There is at least one right, however, which the Son bestows on all humanity, "the [*exousia*] to become the children of God" (John 1:12), and to enjoy "the glorious freedom" of that relationship (Rom. 8:21). Within the larger narrative context of Scripture, the right to become God's children must also mean the right to become more human, the right to participate in the recovery of the divine image conferred on God's children at creation but corrupted through sin. The next three chapters will briefly review some of the ways in which the New Testament story fleshes out this theme and grants additional insight on human rights.

CHRIST AS GOD'S TRUE IMAGE BEARER

The first way it does so is through the fact of incarnation itself. There is a profound hallowing of human worth in the assertion that "the Word became flesh and lived among us" in the person of Jesus Christ (John 1:14). As Karl Barth once said, "The moment God himself became man, man is the measure of all things."[154] We have seen how human dignity proceeds from the creation of Adam, the first earth creature, in the image of God. The fall into sin corrupted but did not erase that image. God's work of redemption is aimed at liberating Adamic humanity from its subjection to evil to fulfill again its appointed role as God's image-bearer, relating openly to God and representing God in the world by living in harmony to God's will.

God's covenant with Israel was a means to this end. But for New Testament faith it is Christ, the Messiah and representative of Israel, who truly achieves this destiny. Where Israel failed, Christ succeeded.

Christ fully manifests the "glory and honor" of human dignity (Heb. 2:5-9; cf. Ps. 8:5-7), and lives in perfect conformity to God's will for human beings (Heb. 10:7, 9; Rom. 5:19). "He is the image of the invisible God, the firstborn of all creation . . . for in him all the fullness of God was pleased to dwell" (Col. 1:15-19; cf. 2 Cor. 4:4). According to Paul, as image bearer *par excellence* Christ becomes "the second man" (1 Cor. 15:47) or the "last Adam" (1 Cor. 15:45; cf. Rom 5:14) who inaugurates a new condition for humanity, one freed from the power and guilt of sin and from the dominion of death (Rom. 6:5-11).

Those who are "in Christ" participate in this new human condition. This new humanity is even now "being renewed in knowledge according to the image of its creator" (Col. 3:10) and will eventually conform perfectly to the image of God's Son (2 Cor. 3:18; 1 Cor. 15:49; Rom. 8:29).[155]

There can be no greater reason for ascribing dignity to human beings than this remarkable claim that the creator God assumed human form, restored the human race to its intended state, and incorporated human experience permanently into God's own life and being. "The more one believes in the mystery of the incarnation," René Coste observes, "the more one's commitment to human rights becomes a matter of motivational urgency."[156]

HUMAN RIGHTS IN THE TEACHING OF JESUS

The supreme value God places on human life also suffuses the historical teaching and activity of Jesus. In the Sermon on the Mount, for example, Jesus reassures his hearers of God's willingness to provide food and clothing by pointing to God's provision for the birds of the air, then asking, "Are you not of more value than they?" (Matt. 6:26). In fending off criticism for allowing his hungry disciples to violate Sabbath law by plucking grain, Jesus declares that "the Sabbath was made for humankind, not humankind for the Sabbath" (Mark 2:27). When challenged over healing on the Sabbath, Jesus points to provisions that allowed for a sheep to be dragged out of a ditch on the Sabbath, then retorts, "How much more valuable is a human being than a sheep!" (Matt. 12:12; cf. Luke 14:5).

This insistence that God's law was intended to liberate rather than enslave human beings lies at the heart of Jesus' conflict with the religious establishment. In Matthew 23, Jesus attacks the scribes and Pharisees for using the law to justify violence and human rights abuse. He accuses them, in effect, of dehumanizing God's law by employing certain of its regulations to "lock people out of the kingdom of heaven" (Matt. 23:13), to exclude human beings from the liberating rule of God rather than striving to include them.

Instead of promoting the justice and freedom of God's reign, they "tie up heavy burdens, hard to bear, and lay them on the shoulders of others, but they themselves are unwilling to lift a finger to move them" (Matt. 23:4). Jesus then tells the Pharisees that the law can only be interpreted rightly when it is viewed from the perspective of its "weightier" demands for "justice, mercy and faith" (Matt. 23:23).

Two things should be noted about this extraordinarily important hermeneutical proposal. The first is the way Jesus prioritizes the Torah's protection of human rights over its requirements for personal piety or ritual purity, even though purity legislation is the single largest component of covenant law. Justice and mercy, Jesus asserts, are more important than meticulous tithing and ceremonial cleanliness. This is both because justice and mercy are to do with upholding the rights and dignity of the disenfranchised, and because a commitment to do so exposes one's true motivations in observing God's law. If obedience to God's will is measured in terms of external purity, motive is irrelevant. If measured in terms of doing justice and showing mercy, inner motivation is of paramount importance. This is why, especially in Matthew's Gospel, Jesus advocates a "hermeneutics of mercy." The Sermon on the Mount opens with the declaration, "blessed are the merciful, for they shall receive mercy" (5:7). Twice Jesus quotes Hosea 6:6, "I desire mercy not sacrifice" (9:13; 12:7). He thus underlines the importance of humanitarian compassion for understanding God's will. Later Jesus tells the Pharisees that all the law and prophets "depend" or "hang" on the double commandment to love God and love one's neighbor as oneself (22:40).

It is the primacy of love and compassion over the letter of the law that explains Jesus' own conduct with respect to the law—his preparedness to eat with sinners, to touch lepers and raise the dead, to heal and harvest on the Sabbath day, and so forth. Mercy is the true meaning of the law; mercy is the heart of God's justice; mercy "fulfills all righteousness" (3:15). Accordingly, as Richard Hays comments, "Those who are trained for the kingdom of heaven are trained to evaluate all norms, even the norms of the law itself, in terms of the criteria of love and mercy. In the community that lives this vision, acts of love and mercy should abound."[157]

The second striking thing about Jesus' hermeneutical statement in Matthew 23:23 is the way "faith" (*pistis*) is mentioned last, not first. The term *pistis* here may designate the ethical quality of honesty or integrity, but more probably it refers to one's relationship to God, demonstrated concretely in faithfulness to God's law. The same ordering of elements is found in Micah 6:8: "He has told you, O mortal, what is good, and what does the Lord require of you but to do justice, and to love kindness, and to walk humbly with your God." A similar pattern occurs in Romans 14:17, where Paul says that "the kingdom of God is not food and drink, but righteousness and peace and joy in the Holy Spirit."

In all three cases, the "spiritual" is mentioned after the "ethical." The clear implication is that one's walk with God,

one's fidelity to God's covenant and knowledge of God's character and being, is fundamentally dependent on doing justice
and showing mercy. It is not that one *first* gets to know God,
then a commitment to justice and mercy follows automatically.
Instead, it is only through doing justice and defending the
poor that true knowledge of God comes (cf. Jer. 9:23; 22:15-16;
Amos 5:21-24; Isa. 58:6). Conversely the real source of defile-
ment is not ritual impurity, as the scribes and Pharisees
thought, but unjust social relationships in which the strong
trample the rights of the weak.

In another interchange with the Pharisees, Jesus explicitly
denies that uncleanness can be ingested with food. He instead
locates the source of contagion in the human heart. As William
Herzog puts it, he sets a prophetic "heart ethic" over against
the Pharisee's "orifice ethics."[158] For it is from the inward motivations of the human heart that flow those sins which truly
assault human dignity, such as murder, adultery, theft, slander, pride, and so on (Mark 7:1-23).

So conscious is Jesus of humanity's right to respect that he
demands his followers root out even thoughts and feelings
that might flare up into acts of murder or revenge or abuse
(Matt. 5:38-48; cf. 1 John 3:15). Even verbal insults are to be
avoided, for Jesus apparently shared the rabbinic view that
deliberately insulting another human being was a terrible sin,
because it was aimed at the victim's dignity as one made in
God's image (Matt. 5:21-26).[159]

Of course the greatest insult to human dignity comes from
deliberately disregarding the right to life. When confronted
with the woman under sentence of death for adultery, Jesus
stoops to draw in the dust, symbolically recalling the common
origin of all human beings as God's creatures made from the
ground in God's image and therefore of unique value (John
7:53-8:11).[160] Jesus indicates that with his appearance on earth
to incarnate God's reign of forgiving justice, any attempt by
self-appointed guardians of God's law to use its provisions to
justify the "legitimate" extinguishing of human life can no
longer to be tolerated.[161]

Jesus' commitment to human rights is demonstrated most
clearly in his ministry to the poor and disadvantaged, those

whose rights were seriously diminished because of religious prejudice or through abusive use of political power. We have seen how covenant law champions the rights of the poor, the weak, the oppressed, and the innocent, and how it was the special task of the king to protect them (Ps. 72:12-13). The royal Messiah was also expected to fulfill this role (Isa. 11:1-10; 61:1-3),[162] and it was precisely this task Jesus set himself at the commencement of his ministry (Luke 4:14-30; 6:20-23; cf. Matt. 25:40).

In the name of God's dawning kingdom, Jesus repeatedly challenged the various discriminations that rendered certain people as outsiders.[163] He did not just avoid negative attitudes to outsiders; he positively affirmed their dignity and welcomed them into his own community. He opposed all discrimination on the basis of race (he healed a Roman centurion's servant) or caste (he affirmed Samaritans), as well as those based on sex (as shown in his treatment of women), age (as displayed in his positive evaluation of children), occupation (he was known as a friend of tax collectors and prostitutes), and social and religious taboos associated with sickness, demon possession, and death.

Jesus so totally identified with the plight of the hungry, the naked, the homeless, and the imprisoned—those denied even the most basic of human rights—that people who acted to relieve their distress, Jesus said, were doing an amazing thing. They were effectively offering personal service to the Messiah and through him to God (Matt. 25:31-46).

Much more could be said about how the values of compassion, forgiveness, sharing, servanthood, equality, justice, and peacemaking which permeate Jesus' teaching and activity imply a commitment to the rights and dignity of all human beings. Under Pharisaic interpretation, the "yoke" of the law was oppressive and dehumanizing. The "yoke" of Jesus was liberating and life-giving. "Come to me, all you that are weary and are carrying heavy burdens and I will give you rest. Take my yoke upon you, and learn from me; for I am gentle and humble in heart, and you will find rest for your souls. For my yoke is easy, and my burden is light" (Matt. 11:28-30).

A LIBERATING DEATH

For the New Testament writers, perhaps even most telling of Jesus' esteem for human worth and human rights was his vicarious, redemptive death. In a striking phrase, the author of Titus characterizes Jesus' saving act as a manifestation of the goodness and "philanthropy" (*philanthropia*) of God, the supreme demonstration of God's immeasurable love for humankind (3:4).

Jesus' treatment at the hands of his enemies was itself a gross violation of human rights. Jesus had lived a life of justice, mercy, and love, a life of fidelity to the true meaning of God's covenant. But in so doing he had challenged the legitimacy of the existing unjust order and threatened those in positions of power, both Jewish and Roman. So they deemed him a dangerous criminal and sought to remove him from the scene. He became a prisoner of conscience. He was falsely accused, unfairly tried, wrongly condemned, brutally tortured, and unjustly executed.[164] Jesus endured "such hostility from sinners against himself" (Heb. 12:3) to break the logic of evil and so win salvation for all of Adam's offspring.

He did so by exposing and absorbing human religious and political violence without retaliation and without compromise.

> He committed no sin, and no deceit was found in his mouth. When he was abused, he did not return abuse; when he suffered, he did not threaten; but he entrusted himself to the one who judges justly. He himself bore our sins in his body on the cross, so that, free from sins, we might live for righteousness. (1 Pet. 2:22-24)

What then is a human being worth? The life blood of God's only Son (cf. Gal. 3:20).

The hideous injustice of Jesus' condemnation and execution is overturned by his resurrection from the dead, where God reverses human "justice" and vindicates Jesus. The resurrection validates Jesus' identity as God's Son and Messiah and confirms his work and way. "The resurrection places God's stamp of approval on the ministry of the prophet of the justice of the reign of God," Herzog explains. "Jesus so embodied that reign that his risen presence is the continuing presence of the reign of God and the constant call for justice 'on earth as it is in heaven.'" Therefore, Herzog continues, "To confess 'Jesus is Lord' is to confess a desire to pursue the vision of justice that informed Jesus' work."[165]

Even after securing liberation for the human race through the death and resurrection of Jesus, God continues to show radical respect for human freedom. Just as Jesus offered but did not impose the kingdom on his hearers (Mark 1:14-15; 10:17-27), so now the saving benefits of Jesus' death and resurrection are offered to people but not imposed coercively on them (Rom. 1:16-17; 10:8-13).

At the same time a new equality of participation is established. The boundaries of the covenant community are redefined. Relationship to Christ rather than commitment to Mosaic law becomes the crucial criterion for membership (Rom. 3:27-31). God's Spirit is now poured out on "all flesh" (Acts 2:17-18), creating a new inclusive, egalitarian community in which the classical sources of human conflict—race, class, wealth, and gender—are to be transcended rather than perpetuated.

This striking egalitarianism is one of the most distinctive and counter-cultural features of the early Jesus movement. It is classically expressed in Galatians 3:28: "There is no longer Jew or Greek, there is no longer slave or free, there is no longer male and female; for all of you are one in Christ Jesus" (cf. 1 Cor. 12:12-13; Rom. 10:12; Col. 3:9-11).

Human dignity and the universality of human rights are thus placed beyond all possible restriction by the universality of redemption in Christ. This universality finds concrete expression in the church, a new kind of human community in which human rights and freedoms can find new levels of realization. To the character and mission of this community we now turn.

7

Church:
Human Rights are
Comprehended in Love
and Freedom

IN CHRIST, GOD REUNITES DIVIDED HUMANITY and so restores the imago Dei on earth. As people are reconciled to God and to one another, true humanization occurs. Not surprisingly, the primary contribution this new inclusive community makes to human rights in a hostile world lies in its ministry of reconciliation (2 Cor. 5:18-20; Eph. 2:11-22). Since people are reconciled to God entirely through grace, all secondary distinctions based on race or ethnic identity, on class or political power, on gender or family membership, are deprived of ultimacy.

By affirming the equality of all in redemption as well as creation, the community of faith was equipped to become a genuinely universal society of human fellowship transcending culturally and socially determined boundaries. The church represented a movement that bonded people together into communities of solidarity whose sole purpose was to promote the reconciliation of people to God and to each other throughout the world. The early church thus functioned as an effective agent for the realization of human rights.[166]

A COMMUNITY OF DIVERSITY AND LOVE

In the New Testament, there are two main keys to the success of the church as a fellowship of reconciliation. The first is a *positive appreciation of diversity.* Genuine solidarity or unity of purpose cannot be achieved by denying or suppressing differences between individuals or between cultures, classes, and genders. There must be room for such differences to flourish, without their becoming or remaining a source of disadvantage. Significantly Paul pictures the church as a "pneumatic democracy."[167] Here the Spirit brings unity precisely by fostering diversity, with each member making different contributions to community life, all of which are equally legitimate and valuable (1 Cor. 12-14; Rom. 12:3-8; Eph. 4:7-16).

Such an understanding enabled the church to function as an agent of renewal within existing social structures that were inherently hierarchical and unjust, such as slavery, patriarchal marriage, and political patronage. New Testament teaching presupposes the continuation of such structures of domination (the church was entirely lacking in power to change them), but concentrates on providing an alternative vision of human relationships within the Christian fellowship.[168] Within this fellowship, "paternalism and proprietorship are to be exchanged for fraternalism and a democratic relationship."[169]

This in turn constituted an indirect challenge to the legitimacy and ultimacy of the hierarchical structures of wider society and an implicit summons to change.[170] Of course this vision of social renewal could not, and did not, become a reality at once. Nurturing diversity without natural or social distinctions becoming a cause of inequity or injustice was a huge challenge, and race, class, wealth, and gender continued to be used by some in the church to justify restricted rights—both within the first generation communities and even more so afterward.

The second key to success, and one that also enabled the first Christians to live within societal structures alien to the spirit of the gospel, is *the priority of love* in all relationships. Communities of reconciliation cannot be achieved simply by enumerating rights to freedom, equality, and solidarity; there must also be an inner momentum driving people to transcend those instincts to self-preservation and private advantage that fuel conflict and competition.

For the first Christians this momentum was supplied by the love of Christ. In his own life and career, Jesus modeled self-giving love (Mark 10:45). In coming to earth, Christ emptied himself of all claims to special privilege and rights to live and die for the benefit of others (Phil. 2:3-7), even his enemies (Rom. 5:6-10).

Those who belong to Christ are repeatedly called to imitate his life of self-sacrifice (e.g., 1 Cor 11:1; 2 Thess. 1:6; 1 Pet. 2:21-25; Heb. 12:3), empowered by the same Spirit who shaped his human character and who now transforms the character of believers into his likeness (Rom. 8:14-17, 26-30). Christ's example of "responsible renunciation,"[171] and the call for believers to emulate such self-denial, provides a radically new, and deeply challenging, perspective for the formation of a Christian attitude to human rights. This Christian attitude contrasts sharply with contemporary conceptions of rights that give priority to individual freedom.

THE CHARACTER OF CHRISTIAN FREEDOM

The notion of freedom has played an influential role in the Western human rights tradition. In the various seventeenth- and eighteenth-century statements on rights and liberties, freedom was largely understood in negative terms—freedom *from* abusive action by the state. The concern was to place limits on arbitrary use of governmental power.

With the steady growth of individualism however, the focus shifted from limiting coercive power to maximizing personal autonomy—positive freedom *for* particular ends. Freedom in contemporary Western culture increasingly means freedom to act on personal preferences, freedom to define one's own standards of behavior, freedom to do what one likes as long as it doesn't hurt anyone else, freedom from anything that limits one's individual choice. As William Stuntz notes,

> The "none-of-your-business-sphere" has grown ever larger, while the sense of moral constraint and obligation to the common good has grown ever weaker. Our society has had quite enough arguing about the virtues of choice. We could stand a good deal more thinking and arguing about which choices are virtuous, and which ones are not.[172]

We have seen how the language and ideal of freedom lies at the heart of the Bible. Freedom of choice is part of this theme. This is evident in the freedom of Adam and Eve to eat of the tree of knowledge in the Garden, the freedom of Israel to choose which god to serve, the freedom of Jesus' hearers to receive or reject his message of the kingdom, the freedom of those who hear the kerygma to accept or reject it. But the Christian view of freedom departs from the contemporary emphasis on freedom as personal autonomy in at least three ways.

Freedom in subjection

To begin with, it is important to note that the essential presupposition for all that is said about freedom in the Bible is humanity's creation by God and continuing dependence on God. This necessarily means that *freedom can never mean absolute autonomy;* it is limited by what is compatible with human creaturehood. True freedom can only be found in being true to ourselves as authentic human beings; it can never come from contradicting our essential humanity. God's gift of freedom, then, is ultimately a freedom to be human, to be the creatures God made us to be. As such it is "freedom in subjection," subjection to the Creator.

For the New Testament writers, the fullest expression of this freedom comes from submission to Christ. "For if the Son makes you free, you will be free indeed" (John 8:36). "For freedom Christ has set us free" (Gal. 5:1). "Where the Spirit of the Lord is there is freedom" (2 Cor. 3:17). But this freedom is not a lordless anarchy in which isolated individuals are free to do whatever their vanity dictates. Freedom is conditioned by its source: union with God in Christ. It can only exist insofar as connection with its nerve center is maintained.

Paul can therefore speak paradoxically of freedom through slavery to Christ (e.g., 1 Cor. 7:22) and slavery "in the new life of the Spirit" (Rom. 7:6). Christians are not their own masters. They have been freed from their old cruel tyrants, and now "belong" to Christ (1 Cor. 6:19-20; 7:23; Gal. 2:19-20; Gal. 3:13-14; Rom. 14:7-8). "If the Old Testament emphasis is on God's people as *freed* slaves," Bauckham comments, "the New Testament emphasis is on God's people as *free* slaves."[173]

Internal and external freedom

Throughout the biblical tradition, freedom is understood principally as *emancipation from oppression*. In the Old Testament, this typically means freedom from *external* oppression—from servitude, forced labor, military opposition, indebtedness, imprisonment, injustice, and so on. The exodus from Egypt and the return from Babylonian exile are paradigmatic in the Old Testament for what freedom means. The New Testament also thinks of freedom in terms of emancipation from external conditions (e.g. Luke 1:67-79; 1 Cor. 7:21-22), but it extends and deepens the conception of freedom to embrace *internal* or moral and spiritual freedom as well—emancipation from the power of sin and guilt, from self-centeredness and alienation, from anxiety and greed, from demons and despair.

This is the dominant referent of liberation language in the New Testament.[174] According to Paul, the inner self is controlled by a range of hostile powers—sin, death, the flesh, desire, and the law—which make for a state of enslavement to the realities of the old age. The gospel liberates by setting people free from the power of sin, the desires of the flesh, the dominion of death, and the condemnation of the law, so that people are free to grow in their relationship with God and to realize their potential as human beings (esp. Rom. 6–8). Such deliverance stands under the "already . . . not yet" tension of Christian eschatology. It is a decisive present experience, but not yet an absolute or completed state. It is continually threatened by the former masters seeking to enslave and subjugate afresh, so it must be constantly guarded and claimed.[175]

God's singular gift of freedom,[176] then, has an outer or sociopolitical dimension (freedom from external constraint) and an inner or spiritual dimension (freedom from internal constraint). One is a freedom of doing, the other a freedom of being. Both can be experienced separately, but both are ultimately required if the freedom to be human—to become the creatures we were made to be—is to be realized.

This deserves emphasis in a climate where rights are appealed to so as to maximize individual freedom. Most human rights function best in the external sphere but have limited impact on the internal sphere (e.g., a right to health care does not free one from neurosis or depression). One may be free from all kinds of external coercion but still have an inner life characterised by despair, anxiety, bad habits, and poor relationships. One may have all one's legal and moral rights respected, and enjoy egalitarian relationships, but still feel unfree.[177]

By contrast, Paul personally experienced a good deal of external opposition (including imprisonment) and his readers had to live out their faith within oppressive and hostile social structures, yet his letters "teem with strong, crisp expressions of a bold, liberated, exalted zest for life."[178] Paul, it seems, regarded interior freedom as a higher or more significant experience than outer freedom. But inward freedom, if it is genuine, *must* affect external relationships. It may enable a person to live joyfully and liberally while externally unfree, but not as a form of passive acquiescence, and never without some immediate change. As a foretaste of God's larger gift of freedom, inner freedom cries out for concrete embodiment in relationships of justice and equality. It implicitly challenges the legitimacy of social and political systems that block and distort human potential, even if in the interim it may have to accept such a contradiction.[179]

Accordingly, a Christian slave could live "as a freed person in the Lord," even though the legal structure of slavery remained intact (1 Cor. 7:22). But when slaves are told to render service willingly as unto Christ (Eph. 6:5-8), and masters are told to render service humbly to their own slaves (!) and treat them as brothers and sisters in Christ (Eph. 6:9; Philm. 16), inner freedom has already begun to subvert outer structures of oppression.[180]

A Christian wife could regard herself as a joint-heir of Christ with her husband, even though patriarchal marriage structures remained in place (1 Pet. 3:7). But when wives are told to submit to their husbands out of love for Christ, not out of a sense of inferiority (Eph. 5:22; Col 3:18), and when Christian husbands are called to love their wives as they do their own bodies (Eph. 5:28; Col 3:19), and even to submit to them in return (Eph. 5:21), gender inequity and patriarchal dominance are effectively doomed.

The priority of love

Third and most important, in Christian thought *freedom is subservient to love.* In the Western liberal tradition, "the only freedom which deserves the name, is that of pursuing our own good in our own way, so long as we do not attempt to deprive others of theirs, or impede their efforts to attain it" (John Stuart Mill). Not so in the Christian tradition: constrained by Christ's love, believers must freely choose to devote their freedom to seeking the good of their neighbor, even at the expense of their own rights and freedom of action. Possessing legitimate rights and freedoms is never sufficient justification for behaving in a certain way; only when such behavior is compatible with the demands of love is it consistent with the will of God revealed in Christ.

This perspective controls Paul's argument in 1 Corinthians 6-10, which contains the most extensive use of rights language (*exousia*, from *exestin*) in the New Testament. In chapter 6, Paul urges the Corinthians not to use their rights (cf. v. 12) to bring lawsuits against each other but to be ready to suffer wrong and be defrauded rather than shame and damage the community.

In chapter 7, Paul reverses the prevailing notion of "conjugal rights" (cf. v. 4) in light of Christian love. The husband does not possess rights of access to his wife, regardless of her feelings. Instead the wife has the right to sexual love and consideration from her husband. Similarly, the wife does not possess rights over her husband; he has the right to expect sexual love and consideration from his partner.

In chapter 8, Paul acknowledges the "freedom" (8:9) of the Corinthian elite to eat food offered to idols. However, he encourages them to forgo this liberty to avoid stumbling weaker members of the congregation. "Knowledge puffs up but love builds up" (8:1).

In chapter 9, Paul discusses his "freedom" and "rights" as a Christian worker. As an apostle, he had "a right to food and drink . . . a right to be accompanied by a believing wife . . . a right to refrain from working for a living" (vv. 4-6). But to avoid putting "an obstacle in the way of the gospel of Christ," he freely renounced his rights (vv. 12, 18; cf. 2 Thess. 3.9).

In chapter 10, he again acknowledges the right (v. 23) of believers to eat whatever they like but encourages them never to "seek their own advantage" (vv. 24, 33). "Be imitators of me," he concludes, "as I am of Christ" (11:1). Christ came not to stand on his rights but to serve others, and surrender his life for the sake of others (Phil. 2:1-11; cf. Mark 10:45).

A similar understanding emerges in Romans 14-15. Here Paul affirms the right of Jewish Christians to act according to their conscience with respect to food laws and holy days and the right of Gentile Christians to follow their own very different convictions on these matters. But because both groups have related to each other on the basis of their rights and freedoms, the Christian community in Rome has sunk into bitterness and division.

Paul therefore advances a different ground for dealing with the issue, the demands of love as exemplified by Christ. "If your brother or sister is being injured by what you eat, you are no longer walking in love. Do not let what you eat cause the ruin of one for whom Christ died. So do not let your good be spoken of as evil" (14:15-16). Instead, "each of us must please our neighbor for the good purpose of building up the neighbor. For Christ did not please himself" (15:2-3). The primary obligation believers owe one another is not non-interference with their rights, but active, considerate love. "Owe no one anything, except to love one another; for the one who loves another has fulfilled the law" (Rom. 13:8; cf. 1 John 3:18).

It must be stressed that this readiness to surrender one's rights and forgo one's freedom for the sake of others is a denial neither of freedom nor of the validity of rights. On the contrary, being free not to exercise freedom is, for Paul, the supreme testimony to his freedom (1 Cor. 9:1). If freedom is absolutized as the ultimate value, one can end up in bondage to freedom, unfree to act in a way that might appear to compromise one's autonomy. When personal freedom is controlled by love, one is truly free.[181]

Similarly, the renunciation of rights presupposes that genuine rights do exist and are legitimate, and that on occasions it is appropriate to claim these rights vigorously (cf. Acts 16:37; 25:11). But where the rights of competing parties come into conflict, Christian love may require one party to waive its rights in order that the rights of the other be upheld. This cannot be an invariable requirement, or else freedom evaporates and justice may suffer. But love of neighbor *is* an obligation for Christians, and love must discern when renunciation of rights is necessary.

CHRISTIAN FREEDOM AND HUMAN RIGHTS

At this point we should pause to consider the implications of this conception of freedom for a Christian approach to human rights. Several considerations commend themselves.

To begin with, the recognition of inner and outer dimensions to freedom underscores, again, the *indivisibility* of human rights. The poor and oppressed have a right to freedom from external oppression and exploitation. They also have a right to be become the children of God (John 1:12) and experience this inner liberation (Rom 8:21). True liberation involves turning against external structures of enslavement *and* turning toward God in faith. For those in the affluent West too, the right to freedom means more than unfettered personal choice; it also means inner liberation from selfishness, sin and greed. Human rights then is not simply about restraining government and securing minimal welfare, it is also about empowering people to orient their lives toward God and their fellow human beings in love and justice.[182]

Again, the biblical subordination of liberty to love suggests a *prioritizing of human rights.* The Western human rights tradition has given greatest weight to freedom; the socialist tradition has stressed equality ahead of individual liberty. Christian tradition places love ahead of both, for love provides the context within which the relative priority of freedom or equality can be determined in specific situations. Love cannot condone rights-claims that allow some to enjoy luxury while others lack food, shelter, and medical care. The right to be free of deprivation deserves precedence over the right to free commerce. The freedom of the market should be subject to the rights of all to the necessities of life and to genuine participation in the community.[183] Indifference to the impact of free trade, for example, on the most vulnerable members of the human family violates the norm of love and debases the concept of freedom.

Emphasis on the sacrifice of one's rights for the sake of others underscores *the limits of a rights-based morality*. Relationships involve more than standing on rights; they require sacrifice, duty, and self-discipline if they are to prosper. Similarly a healthy society cannot function solely on the basis of rights-claims; people must accept obligations, fulfill responsibilities, and show charity. As Marshall observes, "When our responsibilities to one another are couched predominantly in the form of rights, then the principal limit on human conduct that is emphasised is not fairness, or tolerance, or solidarity, or compassion, or charity, but the legal/moral structure of 'rights.'"[184]

Justice gives validity to making rights claims for oneself; it is not inherently selfish to do so but is an expression of one's God-given dignity and a significant contribution to the moral order. But love may mean sacrificing or postponing one's legitimate claims for the sake of others and exercising patience in waiting for others to reciprocate.[185] This seems foreign to much contemporary thinking, but the idea that good can be achieved without self-denial, suffering and sacrifice is entirely foreign to the biblical tradition, and to the Jesus story in particular.[186]

Finally, in giving primacy to the obligation to love (Rom. 13:8) Christian faith challenges both the *privatism* and the *statism* that typify much contemporary rights thinking in our society. Paul Marshall notes how "Many modern rights discussions place an overwhelming emphasis on the human *self.* There is stress on self-preservation, self-development, self-realization, and self-determination."[187] But this "self" is largely understood in isolation from community, and little attention is given to the normative structure of social life. Consequently it is in the individualistic West, where people are increasingly educated in the values of selfishness and self-preservation, that individuals feel most threatened and dissatisfied, most at the mercy of their own solitude.[188]

Such privatism goes hand in hand with a kind of statism inasmuch as there is an almost exclusive focus on state action to secure rights. Government is seen as the primary duty-bearer, responsible to remove as many impediments to personal freedom as possible.[189] Individuals have rights, the government has duties.

This is reflected in Universal Declaration of Human Rights itself. When the document was being framed, several participants urged that it include duties as well as rights. But the president of the Commission, Eleanor Roosevelt, objected vehemently to doing so. The limited reference to duties in the Article 29 was included to satisfy the views of socialist and Latin American writers, and even then it focuses mainly on the duty to respect the rights of others.[190]

But an exaggerated emphasis on political responsibility to enforce human rights, which is increasingly sanctioned by a rapidly growing body of international human rights law that embraces ever broader and more controversial articulations of rights, may itself foster a new kind of totalitarianism. Naming virtually every human good as a right, then requiring governments to provide for them, implies almost limitless governmental power. It also permits governments to infringe virtually any right in the name of supporting other rights named in human rights documents. For this reason, David Smolin fears that the international human rights movement threatens to become "one of the gravest threats to those rights yet conceived by humanity."[191]

In contrast to radical privatism on the one hand and state totalism on the other, the Christian story emphasises persons-in-community. This is why it affirms that obligations and duties are the essential counterpart of rights and freedoms and insists that all people, not just the state, bear duties to the common good. Without a stress on responsibilities, a regime of individual rights generates competition and conflict and provides little incentive to reach across hostile barriers of nationality, class, and culture to create harmony and equality.

Recognition of duties enhances social cohesion, strengthens protection for the vulnerable, and reduces competitive antagonism. But duties without a corresponding stress on rights reduces love of neighbor to paternalism and risks supplanting justice with charity.

When rights and duties are both affirmed, when both are related to a shared vision of the common good, and where individuals avoid exercising rights to the detriment of others and are even prepared to forgo rights for the sake of others, authentic community can emerge. Furthermore, as Martin Shupack points out, such a stance also offers a different way of approaching some of our most divisive social issues. The abortion debate, for example, has largely been conducted in the rhetoric of rights—the rights of the woman versus the rights of the unborn child. An ethos of duty would recast the debate in terms of the relative responsibilities of the parents to the unborn child and of the wider community to the parents and to the child.[192]

So the Christian view of freedom, embodied in a community that honors diversity and nurtures equality, has considerable relevance to the contemporary human rights debate. But the biblical story does not end with the creation of a new community of faith, freedom, and love. In one sense the story is unfinished, for we still live in the time of the church, which still strives, and often fails, to live out this vision of "free love."

In another sense, the biblical narrative does have an end point, a final act, yet to be staged, in which the story of redemption reaches its goal and all creation is brought back fully under the healing reign of God. The various anticipations of this consummation that we find in the New Testament bring with them yet further insight into a Christian understanding of human rights. This is the subject of the next chapter.

8

Consummation: Human Rights Are Vindicated in the Coming Kingdom

T HE GOAL OF GOD'S DEALINGS WITH ISRAEL and the church is the redemption of the entire created order, the consummation of God's sovereignty over all that exists so that "God may be all in all" (1 Cor. 15:28). Hope for the coming reign of God conditions the entire biblical story. The conviction that history under God's supervision is going somewhere, and that the present must be viewed and evaluated in light of the future, is basic to the biblical world view.

This applies as much to its understanding of human dignity and human rights as to everything else: it is an eschatologically qualified ethic. As Moltmann puts it, "Human rights mirror the right of the coming God and the future of humanity."[193] Human rights—conferred at the Creation, frustrated at the Fall, encroached upon by sin, recovered in Christ, and appropriated in the church—shall finally be vindicated in the eschaton.

Such expectancy for the future coming of God to restore creation and confirm the rightful place of humanity in it should energize and inform the Christian commitment to human rights. In this chapter I will briefly consider the importance of hope to human existence, the distinctive character and content of Christian hope, the basis on which the certainty of Christian hope rests, and the implications of Christian eschatology for the doctrine of human rights.

THE IMPORTANCE OF HOPE

Hope is a central component of any life worth living. Individuals need hope to stay healthy, and a healthy society needs a shared sense of social hope to remain confident and purposeful. Hope is also crucially important in the struggle against inhumanity and oppression. As Gary Haugen points out, the battle against injustice is not fought where we often think it is, on the battlefields of power or truth or morality. "In the end the battle against oppression stands or falls on the battlefield of hope."[194] Without hope, without a controlling vision for how things ought to be, and one day *will* be, there is little chance of achieving significant change for the better.

Yet as Duncan Forrester observes, "hope is in crisis in our day."[195] The theme of hope barely surfaces in contemporary theories of justice (or human rights for that matter), and traditional vehicles of hope are in decline. Churches are dwindling, and there is a widespread feeling that utopian political movements, such as Marxism, have been discredited. A vacuum exists, and there seems nothing left to hope for.

In some circles, this "hopelessness" is the outcome of affluence and ease. Western capitalism and liberal democracy have created a culture of complacency and contentment among the well-off, suppressing any need or desire for radical change. Among the poor and dispossessed a different kind of hopelessness prevails. It is the hopelessness of resignation and despair that their predicament will ever be relieved.

Social hope and political idealism have withered, especially on the Western vine; apathy, cynicism and pragmatism have taken over. Whether secularism has the capacity to spawn a rebirth of authentic hope, the kind of hope that will sustain and advance the struggle for the rights and freedoms of all humanity, not just the affluent minority, looks increasingly doubtful.

Christian hope, on the other hand, has generated countless movements of protest, revolution, and reform down through the ages. It has done so by articulating and enacting the biblical belief in the God of justice who is moving history toward its ultimate goal of liberation and renewal, and who stands in judgment over all human structures which hinder his progress or contradict divine goals.

It is this belief that makes Christian hope so politically potent. By envisioning an alternative reality to the one which currently prevails, Christian hope is inherently subversive. It represents a protest against the injustice of the present order of things; it denies the ultimacy or finality of existing social structures and centers of power; it encourages belief in an open future and motivates work for change; and it sustains people through times of suffering and oppression with the reassurance of God's presence in their pain and God's ultimate triumph over all pain (Rev. 21:4).

THE CHARACTER AND CONTENT
OF CHRISTIAN HOPE

The subversive and transformative power of Christian hope all depends, however, on Christian eschatology retaining its authentic, biblical character. If biblical hope is reduced or transposed into something else, it ceases to be true hope and loses its radical edge. Three features of the biblical hope are particularly important in this respect.

First, Christian hope is ultimately *hope in God*, a confidence in the faithfulness of God and in the saving power of God. The coming kingdom is the kingdom *of God*. It is not something we build by our own autonomous efforts but a reality God gives us as a gracious gift. In God's kingdom, humanity finds its fulfillment, but God remains sovereign. Accordingly Christian hope cannot be transposed into a purely secularized or politicized agenda without a serious loss of power and truth.

Christian hope is also profoundly *this-worldly*. It looks for the healing and renewing of this planet, not for its destruction and replacement. For Jesus, the coming of the kingdom means that "God"s will is done *on earth* as it is in heaven" (Matt. 6:10, emph. added). For Paul too, when salvation is complete "creation itself will be set free from its bondage to decay" (Rom. 8:21). The closing scenes of John's Apocalypse depict the "the holy city, the new Jerusalem, coming down out of heaven from God," accompanied by a loud voice announcing God's permanent residence on the earth: "See, the home of God is among mortals; he will dwell with them as their God; they will be his peoples, and God himself will be with them" (Rev. 21:1-4).

Accordingly Christian expectation cannot be reduced to a privatized or spiritualized hope. Christians cannot fix all attention on a heavenly afterlife without seriously impairing the biblical doctrine of creation and promoting escapism or indifference to the social and political needs of this world. Christians are not saved *out of* the world, but *in* the world, *with* the world, indeed *for* the world.

This leads to the third and most important facet of Christian hope: it includes *all creation*, not just humanity, or worse, one small part of it. Just as the entry of sin in the Genesis narratives affects the ground and distorts humanity's relationship with the land, so the final banishment of sin will see the wider created order restored to wholeness. All creation will share in the glorious destiny of redemption. Paul makes this remarkably clear in that classic vision recorded in Romans 8:

> I consider that the sufferings of this present time are not worth comparing with the glory about to be revealed to us. For the creation waits with eager longing for the revealing of the children of God; for the creation was subjected to futility, not of its own will but by the will of the one who subjected it, in hope that the creation itself will be set free from its bondage to decay and will obtain the freedom of the glory of the children of God. We know that the whole creation has been groaning in labor pains until now; and not only the creation, but we ourselves, who have the first fruits of the Spirit, groan inwardly while we wait for adoption, the redemption of our bodies. For in hope we were saved. Now hope that is seen is not hope. For who hopes for what is seen? But if we hope for what we do not see, we wait for it with patience. (Rom. 8:18-25)

The Bible has a paradoxical view of creation. On the one hand, creation sings the glories of God; it reveals the grandeur of its creator. But on the other hand, creation is less than God intends it to be; it has fallen into disorder. In Romans 8, Paul pictures the disorder of creation as a combination of three things: frustration, corruption, and pain (vv. 20-21). It is not just humankind but creation at large that is in bondage to the effects of sin. Suffering, sickness, death, violence, and destruction afflict the whole created order. Yet without minimizing its reality or its intensity, Paul is able to view this affliction in positive terms. The sufferings of creation, he suggests, are like a woman's labor pains, intense but temporary, heralding the dawn of a new creation. This is why the whole passage is shot through with a sense of hope and promise, a joyous confidence in the future. "For I consider that the sufferings of this present time are not worth comparing with the glory about to be revealed to us" (v. 18).

What is this hope for the future, this "glory about to be revealed to us"? Nothing less than the restoration of the entire created order to a condition freed from frustration, death, suffering, and decay.

> Creation itself will be set free from its bondage to decay and will obtain the freedom of the glory of the children of God. We know that the whole creation has been groaning in labor pains [for this to happen] until now. . . . (vv. 21-22)

Paul does not speak of the obliteration of the created order and its replacement with something new. Rather, he speaks of its *liberation* from present slavery to share with humanity in the redemption Christ has wrought. The certainty of this inspires Paul with great hope. He can view present pain positively because knows change is coming, freedom is assured.

THE CERTAINTY OF FUTURE HOPE

But how does Paul know? How can he be so certain? What assurance does he have that this future hope is not a pious fantasy? For Paul, Christian hope is not just wishful thinking. It is based on the concrete experience of what, in v. 23, he calls "the first fruits" of ultimate redemption. Interestingly, in his writings Paul uses the notion of the first-fruits of redemption in connection with three realities, all implicit in Romans 8.

The first is *the resurrection of Jesus.* In 1 Corinthians 15, Paul describes Jesus' bodily resurrection as "the first fruits of those who have died," the first act of the general resurrection (1 Cor.

15:20, 23). Christians can know for sure that God plans to restore the *material* creation because God raised Jesus' *material body* from the dead (hence the empty tomb). Jesus' resurrection is significant not simply because it proves there is life after bodily death but because it inaugurates a new form of bodily life free from subjection to death and decay (Rom. 6:9-10). The bodily (or material) nature of Christ's resurrection serves as the first fruits and guarantee of the ultimate redemption of the bodily (or material) order as a whole. That is why in v. 23 Paul says we can await with confidence "the redemption of our bodies." What happened to Christ will also happen to other human bodies.

Paul also uses the first fruits metaphor for *the gift of Spirit* (Rom. 8:23). For Paul, the Christian age is above all else the age of the Holy Spirit. The eschatological gift of the Spirit achieves liberation from the power of sin and the rule of the law. This gift brings about an inner moral and spiritual renewal, a profound sense of God's love, and a new immediacy of communication with God.[196] But all this represents only "the first-fruits" of what is to come. The "glorious liberty" that God's children now experience in their inner lives and relationships will eventually spill over to the "glorification" of their material bodies as well. "If the Spirit of him who raised Jesus from the dead dwells in you, he who raised Christ from the dead will give life to your mortal bodies also through his Spirit that dwells in you" (Rom. 8:11).

The third application of first fruits in Paul's writings is to *the community of faith.* In 2 Thessalonians 2:13, Paul describes the church as the "first fruits for salvation" (cf. Rom. 11:16). The church, Christ's body, is the first installment of redeemed humanity, a new kind of human community in which the injustices based on class, gender, wealth, and race are to be transcended (Gal. 3:28). The same thought is present in Romans 8: "creation itself will be set free . . . and will obtain the freedom of the glory of the children of God" (v. 21). Non-human creation will share in the liberation which God's children have begun to experience now and will eventually know in fullness.

These three concrete realities—Christ's resurrection, the gift of Spirit, and the existence of the church—give Paul his irrepressible hope and courage in face of the present distress that afflicts God's world. Present agonies are, to the eye of faith, the labor pains of a new, transformed order. The pain is real, but it is also temporary and transitional. A day of liberation is coming, for *all* that God has made.

CHRISTIAN HOPE AND HUMAN RIGHTS

This eschatological framework gives, once again, a distinctive flavor to a Christian perspective on human rights. It provides, for example, a firm foundation for so-called "future rights"—the rights of unborn generations to a share in the earth's resources and benefits. Advocates of future rights propose that the current generation has the earth on loan. It has been passed on to us by our ancestors, and we hold it in trust for our descendants, who consequently have a claim on us with respect to their inheritance.[197]

Christian eschatology takes us one step further however. The earth is not only the inheritance of the next generation, it is the future inheritance of the present and past generations as well. Christian hope is all-inclusive. Materiality will be redeemed, and all humanity are heirs of God's redeemed earth. All generations have a "right" to the future.

This in turn means that all are responsible to live now in a manner that is consistent with, and even contributes to, the realization of the future environment. For a Christian, ecological duties are motivated not simply by enlightened self-interest, or even by the claims of the next generation, but by the claim of God to his own creation, God's "right" to what God has made and restored in Christ. That "all things in heaven and on earth" were created through Christ and for Christ (Col. 1:15-20) and "all things . . . , things in heaven and things on earth," will be "gathered up in him" (Eph. 1:10) is the ultimate, and the only necessary, justification for Christian recognition of "ecological rights." To love creation's Lord is to love the Lord's creation and acknowledge its rightful destiny.

This destiny, however, is assured only because human dignity and human rights are an enduring reality that God honors. Humanity has no right to salvation in the sense of deserving it. But God's commitment to his covenant with the human race, under which human rights are given, is unfaltering (Rom. 3:1-4), and so salvation is secured. Paul describes the experience of salvation as one of liberation, and it is this human experience of freedom that guarantees ecological survival. "For the creation itself will be set free from its bondage to decay and will obtain the freedom of the glory of the children of God" (Rom. 8:21-22). From this perspective, human rights and environmental rights are inextricably united.

The distinctive feature of New Testament eschatology is the conviction that God's awaited reign has already commenced in the present. The kingdom has already come, in Jesus, but it has not yet come in its fullness.[198] This also gives a distinctive twist to Christian human rights thinking. It means no system of human or environmental rights can be accorded absolute value. All are provisional and all stand under the judgment of God, accountable to God's will and purpose. Christians owe ultimate allegiance to Christ's kingdom alone and look finally to him to secure human rights.

This is not to justify political quietism or detachment from human and ecological rights in the world today. Quite the contrary. Biblical accounts of the redemption of creation are not only intended to inspire hope but also to incite action, to inspire actions that are consistent with our future hope for a renewed earth, freed from destruction, violence, and injustice. Just as faith without works is dead, so hope without action is, simply, hopeless! Hope is more than an attitude of otherworldly optimism. Hope finds feet in deeds of commitment that both anticipate (or point toward) what we hope for, and even, in the grace of God, contribute toward its realization. W. Sibley Towner captures this point well:

> We need to think . . . clearly about the future of nature and the role we are to play. . . . If that future is going to be characterized by wholeness, we have to work hard for it now. Like magnets . . . idealistic visions of a perfected nature pull us toward them . . . because they have moral authority. They enable us to engage in proleptic action now. If peace is the hallmark of the new age (Isa. 11:1-9), then our work in this time of tribulation is to abolish war and to effect reconciliation between people, as well as between people, wolves, and snakes. If abundance of life, taken now to mean both

quality of life and bio-diversity, is manifested in the Eden ahead (Ezek. 34:25-31), then we can do nothing better now than to attend to the rain forests (Gen. 2:5, 15), cut back on over-consumption, and limit the growth of the human population. We will continue to use nature, of course, but no longer threaten to use it up. If the nature that lies along the banks of the River of Life is spotlessly beautiful (Ezek. 47:1-12; Rev. 22:1-2), then our path to action turns away from waste, pollution, using up the earth's resources. . . . The biblical pictures of nature in the future function as incitements toward a style of ethical living in the present that is wholistic, interdependent, non-hierarchical, and one that does not reject flesh and matter as corrupt because God does not reject them.[199]

In undertaking such actions, Christians will join forces with other people of good will. Their actions will often be similar. But their understanding of what they are doing, and why they are doing it, will be different. Christians should care for the environment, oppose militarism, avoid waste, and champion human rights as a witness to and a celebration of God's passionate love for all that God has made and of God's promise to put right all that has gone wrong on earth.

Human action, on its own, will not bring about the new creation; that is God's work which God will accomplish in God's own good time. But that fact is not meant to paralyze us, to render us as mere spectators on God's work in world. Our deeds of justice will act as concrete demonstrations of what God is going to do, and in fact is already doing now, partly through these deeds themselves.

It is the character, content, and certainty of biblical hope, then, that informs and energizes a Christian perspective on human rights. "Abounding in hope by the power of the Holy Spirit" (Rom. 15:13), Christians should work ceaselessly for human and environmental rights, freed from manipulation by lesser loyalties, expectant of miracles (the kingdom is here) but realistic about what can be achieved (the kingdom is not yet fully here), always mindful that "human beings do not live by bread alone, but by every word that comes from the mouth of God" (Matt. 4:4; Deut. 8:3).

9

Conclusion

THE BIBLE DOES NOT CONTAIN a fully elaborated, codified doctrine of human rights. We owe that development largely to the post-Enlightenment Western secular tradition. But that tradition was built on a world view and value system deeply conditioned by the Christian faith and by the biblical story in particular. Without the influence of that story, it is doubtful if human rights instruments like the Universal Declaration of Human Rights would have ever emerged.

Secularism however declared its independence from, even opposition to, the Christian tradition, not least because of the oppressive record of the institutional church. In consequence, secular human rights doctrine is better able to assert human dignity and human rights than to explain or justify them.

A biblically informed account, by contrast, offers the most profound justification for the ascription of dignity and rights to human beings—they have been made in the image of God, occupying a place "a little lower than God" (Ps. 8:5, cf. Heb. 2:7). They have been crowned with glory and honor and are the object of God's love and redemptive activity, with God taking on human nature (John 1:14) so that humans "may become participants of the divine nature" (2 Pet. 1:4).

As well as offering a unique justification for human rights, the biblical tradition offers a distinctive perspective on the content and character of human rights. It would be repetitive, after such a long journey through the biblical narrative, to summarize these distinctive features here. Let me simply suggest that the three dimensions of the divine image identified in my discussion of creation (chapter 3) capture the essence of this distinctiveness.

In both idiom and emphasis, the Bible stresses the primacy of *responsibility* in human rights. Human beings are called to conform their lives and relationships to the will of God, which includes taking responsibility for the welfare of their sisters and brothers. This entails more than non-interference with their freedoms and rights; it requires practical concern for and positive action on behalf of others, especially the poor and the oppressed.[200]

The biblical emphasis on duty and obligation should cause us to question the wisdom of casting so many of the issues of modern social life solely in terms of rights. Rights and responsibilities are complementary and indivisible in the biblical tradition: rights are the outworking of responsibility. This means that one-sided emphasis on either category will inevitably lead to distortion.

Modernity's concern with rights was a needed corrective to the totalitarian stress on obligation in the premodern period. In many parts of the globe today, there is still an urgent need to champion human rights against abusive regimes that employ the instruments of oppression to exact unjust duties from their population. But arguably the pendulum has swung too far in the individualistic, postmodern West. There is need to recover the meaning of "social responsibility" and the "common good." We cannot but be our brother's and sister's keeper.

The biblical tradition also accents the *relational* character of human rights. Whereas the secular tradition understands rights as inherent within autonomous individuals, in the Bible it is persons-in-community that have rights and bear duties. Robert Gascoigne captures this contrast well:

> The liberal conception of autonomy has as its highest value the free self-disposition of the self-aware individual agent. For the Christian tradition, the fullest expression of this free self-disposition is in the realization of the individual through relationships of mutual commitment: relationships to God as the source of human life and to other persons as the essential context for personal fulfilment. Freedom is understood as the possibility of fulfilment through

relationships of community, rather than, as in the secular
liberal tradition, the absence of any warrantable and justified claims on the individual's autonomy.[201]

Human personality is always viewed in the Bible in relational terms: one cannot be human alone. To be human is to
be in relationship to God and to other people. All rights and
responsibilities derive from this fact. This gives equal validity
to individual and communal rights and duties and underscores their inseparable connection. It also highlights the priority of love over personal rights and freedoms, something
strongly emphasized in New Testament teaching.

If human rights claims in contemporary Western society
are increasingly characterized by a "morally aimless liberty
and the clash of self-centered private interests,"[202] in biblical
perspective rights must serve relationships, both personal and
social. This means rights should not be isolated from all the
other ingredients necessary for healthy relations. Relationships flourish not on the basis of a legally compelled acknowl-
edgment of mutual rights but on "countless acts of unre-
quested goodwill."[203] The parties must accept obligations,
honor commitments, show compassion, and go the second
mile.

Rights are still crucially important to relationships,[204] and
Christians should promote them. But Christians should perhaps resist the current imperialism of rights-talk, because it
encourages a reductionist view of relationships and obscures
the fact that people's deepest human needs—for love, joy, forgiveness, intimacy, and comfort—cannot be demanded as
rights but must be received as gifts.[205]

Finally, in the biblical tradition human rights have a *repre-
sentational* character—they represent the character of the
"right-eous" God in whose image human beings are made.
They equip humans to represent that God in exercising rule
over the earth. Rights are not deductions made on the basis of
abstract notions of equality, freedom or justice. They are expressions of what God is like, as revealed in historical acts of
deliverance. Rights represent the justice of God.

This gives particular content to key human rights values.
Equality is not treating all people exactly the same but com-

pensating for disability, natural or social, so that the poor and the oppressed, who possess equal dignity as God's image-bearers, are not deprived of access to and participation in the benefits of creation. Freedom is not freedom *from* subjection to all restrictions but freedom *in* subjection to God's will. Justice is not giving each person their due but maintaining and restoring relationship.[206]

Rights also represent the rule of God. In biblical perspective, environmental and ecological rights and duties have unique grounding in the doctrine of creation and in the hope for the coming kingdom. And it is the dawning of that kingdom, the day when "God's will is done on earth as it is in heaven," that will finally see the rights of God's children and of all God's creatures to "glorious liberty" (Rom. 8:21) finally fulfilled. To that end we should work and pray.

Appendix

The Universal Declaration of Human Rights

On December 10, 1948, the General Assembly of the United Nations adopted and proclaimed the Universal Declaration of Human Rights, the full text of which appears in the following pages. Following this historic act the Assembly called on all member countries to publicize the text of the Declaration and "to cause it to be disseminated, displayed, read and expounded principally in schools and other educational institutions, without distinction based on the political status of countries or territories."

PREAMBLE

Whereas recognition of the inherent dignity and of the equal and inalienable rights of all members of the human family is the foundation of freedom, justice and peace in the world,

Whereas disregard and contempt for human rights have resulted in barbarous acts which have outraged the conscience of mankind, and the advent of a world in which human beings shall enjoy freedom of speech and belief and freedom from fear and want has been proclaimed as the highest aspiration of the common people,

Whereas it is essential, if man is not to be compelled to have recourse, as a last resort, to rebellion against tyranny and oppression, that human rights should be protected by the rule of law,

Whereas it is essential to promote the development of friendly relations between nations,

Whereas the peoples of the United Nations have in the Charter reaffirmed their faith in fundamental human rights, in the dignity and worth of the human person and in the equal rights of men and women and have determined to promote social progress and better standards of life in larger freedom,

Whereas Member States have pledged themselves to achieve, in co-operation with the United Nations, the promotion of universal respect for and observance of human rights and fundamental freedoms,

Whereas a common understanding of these rights and freedoms is of the greatest importance for the full realization of this pledge,

Now, Therefore THE GENERAL ASSEMBLY proclaims THIS UNIVERSAL DECLARATION OF HUMAN RIGHTS as a common standard of achievement for all peoples and all nations, to the end that every individual and every organ of society, keeping this Declaration constantly in mind, shall strive by teaching and education to promote respect for these rights and freedoms and by progressive measures, national and international, to secure their universal and effective recognition and observance, both among the peoples of Member States themselves and among the peoples of territories under their jurisdiction.

ARTICLE 1

All human beings are born free and equal in dignity and rights.They are endowed with reason and conscience and should act toward one another in a spirit of brotherhood.

ARTICLE 2

Everyone is entitled to all the rights and freedoms set forth in this Declaration, without distinction of any kind, such as race, colour, sex, language, religion, political or other opinion, national or social origin, property, birth or other status. Furthermore, no distinction shall be made on the basis of the political, jurisdictional or international status of the country or territory to which a person belongs, whether it be independent, trust, non-self-governing or under any other limitation of sovereignty.

ARTICLE 3
Everyone has the right to life, liberty and security of person.

ARTICLE 4
No one shall be held in slavery or servitude; slavery and the slave trade shall be prohibited in all their forms.

ARTICLE 5
No one shall be subjected to torture or to cruel, inhuman or degrading treatment or punishment.

ARTICLE 6
Everyone has the right to recognition everywhere as a person before the law.

ARTICLE 7
All are equal before the law and are entitled without any discrimination to equal protection of the law. All are entitled to equal protection against any discrimination in violation of this Declaration and against any incitement to such discrimination.

ARTICLE 8
Everyone has the right to an effective remedy by the competent national tribunals for acts violating the fundamental rights granted him by the constitution or by law.

ARTICLE 9
No one shall be subjected to arbitrary arrest, detention or exile.

ARTICLE 10
Everyone is entitled in full equality to a fair and public hearing by an independent and impartial tribunal, in the de-

termination of his rights and obligations and of any criminal charge against him.

ARTICLE 11

(1) Everyone charged with a penal offence has the right to be presumed innocent until proved guilty according to law in a public trial at which he has had all the guarantees necessary for his defence.

(2) No one shall be held guilty of any penal offence on account of any act or omission which did not constitute a penal offence, under national or international law, at the time when it was committed. Nor shall a heavier penalty be imposed than the one that was applicable at the time the penal offence was committed.

ARTICLE 12

No one shall be subjected to arbitrary interference with his privacy, family, home or correspondence, nor to attacks upon his honor and reputation. Everyone has the right to the protection of the law against such interference or attacks.

ARTICLE 13

(1) Everyone has the right to freedom of movement and residence within the borders of each state.

(2) Everyone has the right to leave any country, including his own, and to return to his country.

ARTICLE 14

(1) Everyone has the right to seek and to enjoy in other countries asylum from persecution.

(2) This right may not be invoked in the case of prosecutions genuinely arising from non-political crimes or from acts contrary to the purposes and principles of the United Nations.

ARTICLE 15

(1) Everyone has the right to a nationality.

(2) No one shall be arbitrarily deprived of his nationality nor denied the right to change his nationality.

ARTICLE 16

(1) Men and women of full age, without any limitation due to race, nationality or religion, have the right to marry and to found a family. They are entitled to equal rights as to marriage, during marriage and at its dissolution.

(2) Marriage shall be entered into only with the free and full consent of the intending spouses.

(3) The family is the natural and fundamental group unit of society and is entitled to protection by society and the State.

ARTICLE 17

(1) Everyone has the right to own property alone as well as in association with others.

(2) No one shall be arbitrarily deprived of his property.

ARTICLE 18

Everyone has the right to freedom of thought, conscience and religion; this right includes freedom to change his religion or belief, and freedom, either alone or in community with others and in public or private, to manifest his religion or belief in teaching, practice, worship and observance.

ARTICLE 19

Everyone has the right to freedom of opinion and expression; this right includes freedom to hold opinions without interference and to seek, receive and impart information and ideas through any media and regardless of frontiers.

ARTICLE 20

(1) Everyone has the right to freedom of peaceful assembly and association.

(2) No one may be compelled to belong to an association.

ARTICLE 21

(1) Everyone has the right to take part in the government of his country, directly or through freely chosen representatives.

(2) Everyone has the right of equal access to public service in his country.

(3) The will of the people shall be the basis of the authority of government; this will shall be expressed in periodic and genuine elections which shall be by universal and equal suffrage and shall be held by secret vote or by equivalent free voting procedures.

ARTICLE 22
Everyone, as a member of society, has the right to social security and is entitled to realization, through national effort and international co-operation and in accordance with the organization and resources of each State, of the economic, social and cultural rights indispensable for his dignity and the free development of his personality.

ARTICLE 23
(1) Everyone has the right to work, to free choice of employment, to just and favorable conditions of work and to protection against unemployment.

(2) Everyone, without any discrimination, has the right to equal pay for equal work.

(3) Everyone who works has the right to just and favorable remuneration ensuring for himself and his family an existence worthy of human dignity, and supplemented, if necessary, by other means of social protection.

(4) Everyone has the right to form and to join trade unions for the protection of his interests.

ARTICLE 24
Everyone has the right to rest and leisure, including reasonable limitation of working hours and periodic holidays with pay.

ARTICLE 25
(1) Everyone has the right to a standard of living adequate for the health and well-being of himself and of his family, including food, clothing, housing and medical care and necessary social services, and the right to security in the event of unemployment, sickness, disability, widowhood, old age or other lack of livelihood in circumstances beyond his control.

(2) Motherhood and childhood are entitled to special care and assistance. All children, whether born in or out of wedlock, shall enjoy the same social protection.

ARTICLE 26

(1) Everyone has the right to education. Education shall be free, at least in the elementary and fundamental stages. Elementary education shall be compulsory. Technical and professional education shall be made generally available and higher education shall be equally accessible to all on the basis of merit.

(2) Education shall be directed to the full development of the human personality and to the strengthening of respect for human rights and fundamental freedoms. It shall promote understanding, tolerance and friendship among all nations, racial or religious groups, and shall further the activities of the United Nations for the maintenance of peace.

(3) Parents have a prior right to choose the kind of education that shall be given to their children.

ARTICLE 27

(1) Everyone has the right freely to participate in the cultural life of the community, to enjoy the arts and to share in scientific advancement and its benefits.

(2) Everyone has the right to the protection of the moral and material interests resulting from any scientific, literary or artistic production of which he is the author.

ARTICLE 28

Everyone is entitled to a social and international order in which the rights and freedoms set forth in this Declaration can be fully realized.

ARTICLE 29

(1) Everyone has duties to the community in which alone the free and full development of his personality is possible.

(2) In the exercise of his rights and freedoms, everyone shall be subject only to such limitations as are determined by law solely for the purpose of securing due recognition and re-

spect for the rights and freedoms of others and of meeting the just requirements of morality, public order and the general welfare in a democratic society.

(3) These rights and freedoms may in no case be exercised contrary to the purposes and principles of the United Nations.

ARTICLE 30

Nothing in this Declaration may be interpreted as implying for any State, group or person any right to engage in any activity or to perform any act aimed at the destruction of any of the rights and freedoms set forth herein.

Notes

FOREWORD

1. Stassen, "Michael Walzer's Situated Justice," *Journal of Religious Ethics* (Fall, 1994).

2. H. E. Tödt and Wolfgang Huber, *Menschenrechte [Human Rights]*, (Stuttgart, Germany: Kreuz Verlag, 1977), l8ff., 52; Tödt, *Perspektiven Theologischer Ethik* (Munich, Germany: Christian Kaiser Verlag, 1988), 104f., and chapter 7.

3. David Gushee, *Righteous Gentiles of the Holocaust* (Minneapolis: Augsburg Fortress 1994).

4. Glen Stassen, *Just Peacemaking: Transforming Initiatives for Justice and Peace* (Louisville: Westminster John Knox: 1992), chapter 6. Michael Westmoreland-White has developed the argument further, showing biblical roots for human rights, as well as human-rights affirmation in Athenagoras, St. Basil, and St. John Chrysostom in the Eastern Church. David Hollenbach, *Claims in Conflict: Retrieving and Renewing the Catholic Human Rights Tradition* (New York: Paulist Press: 1979) and Max Stackhouse, *Creeds, Society, and Human Rights* (Grand Rapids, Mich.: Eerdmans: 1984) show origins of human rights in medieval Catholic and free church Puritan political theory.

CROWNED WITH GLORY AND HONOR

1. The proceedings of that conference have been published in B. Atkin and K. Evans (eds.), *Human Rights and the Common Good: Christian Perspectives* (Wellington: Victoria University Press, 1999). The present book is a revised version of my contribution to that collection.

2. This is based on the research of Kevin Bales, University of Surrey, as reported in the *New Zealand Herald*, December 4, 2000.

3. Reported in the *New Zealand Herald*, February 20, 2001.

4. K. Belgrave, *New Zealand Herald*, February 20, 2001.

5. G. George, *New Zealand Herald*, January 18, 2001.

6. F. Haden, *Sunday Star Times*, December 3, 2000.

7. Exod. 21:10; Deut. 22:30; 27:20; 1 Sam. 10:25; Prov. 29:7; 31:5, 8, 9; Isa. 5:23; Jer. 5:28; Lam. 3:35; 1 Cor. 7:3; 9:15, 18; cf. also Job 36:6; Ps. 82:3; Eccl. 5:8; Isa. 10:2.

8. Whether the distinctiveness of Christian ethics lies in its content (i.e., it offers a distinct conception of the good) or merely in the motivations it supplies for performing the good, is a matter of debate. On the relationship of this debate to rights, see K. Cronin, *Rights and Christian Ethics* (Cambridge, England: Cambridge University Press, 1992), 233-50.

9. See Cronin, *Rights and Christian Ethics*, 26-56; B. Almond, "Rights," in P. Singer (ed.), *A Companion To Ethics* (Oxford: Blackwell, 1991), 261-62; J. W. Montgomery, *Human Rights and Human Dignity* (Grand Rapids, Mich.: Zondervan, 1986), 60-80; J. Rivers, "The Virtue of Rights," *Studies in Christian Ethics* 13/2 (2000): 67-90

10. Freedom is sometimes used negatively (freedom from) and sometimes positively (freedom for), and is appealed to both to protect rights (e.g., free elections) and to justify the neglect of rights (e.g., free market economics). Equality can refer to equality of opportunity, of access, of action, of outcome, or of inherent worth or dignity. Equality requires that like cases be treated alike and different cases be treated differently. But this requires deciding which likenesses are relevant likenesses and which differences are relevant differences. This is often a subjective judgment, and the concept is therefore open to manipulation by particular interest groups.Moreover freedom and equality may sometimes contradict one another. Does freedom, for example, include the freedom to be unequal?

11. On reasons for such philosophical skepticism, see Cronin, *Rights and Christian Ethics*, 57-80.

12. M. Shupack, "The Demands of Dignity *and* Community: An Ecumenical and Mennonite Account of Human Rights," *Conrad Grebel Review* (Fall, 1996): 243; idem, "The Churches and Human Rights: Catholic and Protestant Human Rights Views as Reflected in Church Statements," *Harvard Human Rights Journal* 6 (1993): 128.

13. This is a necessary postulate, since if rights are tied to the capacity or necessity of laying claim to them, groups such as infants, children and the intellectually impaired are automatically disenfranchised. Logically there is also a difference between rightly claiming something and having a right.

14. P. Marshall, "Justice and Rights: Ideology and Human Rights Theories," in S. Griffiden and J. Verhoegt (eds.), *Mirror and Context in the Social Sciences* (Lanham, Md.: University Press of America, 1990), 139-44.

15. For an excellent discussion on the continuity between natural rights and recent formulations of human rights, see D. Sidorsky, "Contemporary Reinterpretations of the Concept of Human Rights," in D. Sidorsky (ed.), *Essays on Human Rights: Contemporary Issues and Jewish Perspectives* (Philadelphia: The Jewish Publication Society of America, 1979), 92-95.

16. K. Vasak (ed.), *The International Dimensions of Human Rights* 2 vols. (English Translation: Westport, Conn.: Greenwood Press, 1982).

17. Cf. P. Marshall, "Does the Creation Have Rights?," *Studies in Christian Ethics* 6/2 (1993): 31-49.

18. See Sidorsky, "Contemporary Reinterpretations," 104ff.

19. "Personal civil and political freedom mean very little if one is suffering poverty and privation or is living in a situation of inequality or economic exploitation. By the same token, social, economic and cultural rights and freedoms are hollow achievements if unaccompanied by personal freedom, rights and duties. Liberty absent justice is vain; justice absent liberty is false. True liberty and true justice presuppose one another," J. D. Gort, "The Christian Ecumenical Reception of Human Rights," in A. A. An-Na'im, et al. (eds.), *Human Rights and Religious Values: An Uneasy Relationship?* (Grand Rapids, Mich.: Wm B. Eerdmans, 1995), 224.

20. M. Stackhouse, *Creeds, Society and Human Rights: A Study in Three Cultures* (Grand Rapids, Mich.: Wm. B. Eerdmans 1984), 1.

21. On this, see A. F. Droogers, "Cultural Relativism and Universal Human Rights?," in An-Na'im, *Human Rights and Religious Values,* 79-80.

22. F. Wilfred, "The Language of Human Rights: An Ethical Esperanto?," in R. S. Sugirtharajah (ed.), *Frontiers in Asian Christian Theology: Emerging Trends* (Maryknoll, N.Y.: Orbis, 1994), 213.

23. D. B. Forrester, *Christian Justice and Public Policy* (Cambridge: Cambridge University Press, 1997), 45, cf. 187-88.

24. For an analysis of the impact of such philosophical developments on literary interpretation in general, and biblical studies in particular, see A. C. Thiselton, *New Horizons in Hermeneutics: The Theory and Practice of Transforming Biblical Reading* (Grand Rapids, Mich.: Zondervan, 1992). I am also grateful for the insights contained in two unpublished papers by M. A. King, "Standing on Something: Incipient Foundationalism in the Sophistic Rhetoric of Rorty, Fish and Hernstein Smith," and "Standing on Something Part 2: From Rorty's Solidarity Against Objectivity to Gadamer's Solidarity as Objectivity".

25. Even if "objectivism" in the old Enlightenment sense is no longer plausible, complete subjectivism or relativism is, ultimately, an impossible alternative. What is needed is some form of critical or perspectival realism that allows *both* for the giveness of truth (or human rights) *and* for the partial or contextual nature of all human apprehensions and articulations of truth (or rights).

26. Wilfred, "The Language of Human Rights": 206-20.

27. Cf. Stackhouse, *Creeds, Society and Human Rights,* 267-77.

28. As in J. Clayton, "Religions and Rights: Local Values and Universal Declarations," in An-Na'im, *Human Rights and Religious Values,* 264.

29. If rationality is entirely derived from culture, there would be no rational basis for critiquing irrationality, with cultural relativism producing the kind of ethnocentrism it were intended to prevent. Some of the criteria of rationality are context-dependent, but others are universal, intelligible to all cultures. See Droogers, "Cultural Relativism," 83.

30. Clayton identifies five different strategies that have been used to

bridge between local religious traditions and universal human rights, "Religions and Rights," 261-63. See also Shupack, "The Churches and Human Rights," 147-49.

31. For a sustained argument that it is still possible in the context of postmodern cultural consciousness to arrive at common insight into the human condition through dialogue between traditions, see R. Gascoigne, *The Public Forum and Christian Ethics* (Cambridge: Cambridge University Press, 2001), esp. 163-211.

32. Stackhouse, *Creeds, Society and Human Rights*, 271.

33. Cf. T. Koontz, "Are Human Rights Universal? A Response," *MCC Peace Office Newsletter* 25/3 (1995): 3-5.

34. J. Barr, "Ancient Biblical Laws and Modern Human Rights," in D.A. Knight and P. J. Peters (eds.), *Justice and the Holy: Essays in Honor of Walter Harrelson* (Atlanta: Scholars Press, 1989), 22, 23.

35. See, for example, P. de Rosa, *Vicars of Christ: The Dark Side of the Papacy* (London: Corgi Books, 1988).

36. Cf. D. Tutu, "Religion and Human Rights," in H. Küng (ed.), *Yes to a Global Ethic* (London: SCM, 1996), 164-174.

37. Cf. R. Gill, *Moral Communities* (Exeter: University of Exeter Press, 1992), 42-85; idem, *Moral leadership in a Postmodern Age* (Edinburgh: T & T Clark, 1997), 154-60.

38. Clayton, "Religions and Rights," 266.

39. As in Clayton, "Religions and Rights," 268; M. Shupack, "The Churches and Human Rights: Catholic and Protestant Human Rights Views as Reflected in Church Statements," *Harvard Human Rights Journal* 6 (1993): 153.

40. Heb 10:16; 2 Cor 3:6; cf. Jer 31:30; Prov 3:3; 7:3.

41. Clayton, "Religions and Rights," 260.

42. Stackhouse, *Creeds, Society and Human Rights*, 107.

43. See, for example, J. Langan, "Human Rights in Roman Catholicism," *Journal of Ecumenical Studies* 19/3 (1982): 25-39; J. R. Meyer, "Human Rights, Fact or Fiction? 'Human Rights and the 'Risk of Freedom,'" *SJT* 52 (1999): 49-81.

44. See, for example, J. T. E. Renner and V. C. Pfitzner, "Justice and Human Rights: Some Biblical Perspectives," *Lutheran Theological Journal* 24/1 (1990): 3-10.

45. See, for example, A. van Egmond, "Calvinist Thought and Human Rights," in A. A. An-Na'im, et al. (eds.), *Human Rights and Religious Values: An Uneasy Relationship?* (Grand Rapids, Mich.: Wm. B. Eerdmans, 1995), 192-202.

46. Cf. I. Ellacuriía and J. Sobrino (eds.), *Mysterium Liberationis: The Fundamental Concepts of Liberation Theology* (Maryknoll: Orbis, 1993); M. Eastham, "A Critique of the Human Rights Tradition from the Writings of Gustavo Gutiérrez: 1974-1979," in B. Atkin and K. Evans (eds.), *Human Rights and the Common Good: Christian Perspectives* (Wellington, New Zealand: Victoria University Press, 1999), 77-96.

47. See especially Shupack, "The Churches and Human Rights," 127-57; J. D. Gort, "The Christian Ecumenical Reception of Human Rights,"

in A. A. An-Na'im, et al. (eds.), *Human Rights and Religious Values: An Uneasy Relationship?* (Grand Rapids, Mich.: Wm. B. Eerdmans, 1995), 203-28; J. Moltmann, *On Human Dignity: Political Theology and Ethics* (Philadelphia: Fortress Press, 1984), 3-18.

48. D. B. Forrester, "Political Justice and Christian Theology," *Studies in Christian Ethics* 3/1 (1990): 5; cf. idem, *Christian Justice and Public Policy*, 9-37.

49. See C. D. Marshall, "The Use of the Bible in Ethics: Scripture, Ethics, and the Social Justice Statement," in J. Boston and A. Cameron (eds.), *Voices for Justice: Church, Law and State In New Zealand* (Palmerston North, New Zealand: Dunmore Press, 1994), 107-146.

50. J.C. Swaim, "Bible Proclamation of Human Rights," *International Journal of Religious Education* 44 (1968): 4.

51. C. Sugden, "The Right to be Human: Four Bible Studies," *Religion and Society* 19/2 (1982): 47.

52. J. R. Nelson, "Human Rights in Creation and Redemption: A Protestant View," *Journal of Ecumenical Studies* 19/3 (1982): 10; also Renner and Pfitzner, "Justice and Human Rights": 7.

53. See Montgomery, *Human Rights*, 168-69; Swaim, "Bible Proclamation," 4-5.

54. E. Pagels, "The Roots and Origins of Human Rights," in R. B. McKay and H. Cleveland (eds.), *Human Dignity: The Internationalization of Human Rights* (Dobbs Ferry, N.Y.: Oceana Publishing, 1979), 1-8.

55. Barr, "Ancient Biblical Laws," 21-33 (quote from p. 28).

56. H. C. Brichto, "The Hebrew Bible on Human Rights," in D. Sidorsky (ed.), *Essays on Human Rights: Contemporary Issues and Jewish Perspectives* (Philadelphia: The Jewish Publication Society of America, 1979), 216.

57. Brichto, "Hebrew Bible," 220.

58. L. Henkin, "Judaism and Human Rights," *Judaism* 25/4 (1976): 436-37; R. Cassin, "From the Ten Commandments to the Rights of Man," in Shlomo Shoham (ed.), *Of Law and Man: Essays in Honor of Haim H. Cohn* (New York: Sabra Books, 1971), 13-18.

59. So D. F. Polish, "Judaism and Human Rights," *Journal of Ecumenical Studies* 19/3 (1982): 40.

60. Stackhouse, *Creeds, Society and Human Rights*, 31; cf. D. A. Knight, "The Ethics of Human Life in the Hebrew Bible," in D. A. Knight and P. J. Peters (eds.), *Justice and the Holy: Essays in Honor of Walter Harrelson* (Atlanta: Scholars Press, 1989), 65-88.

61. Barr, "Ancient Biblical Laws," 21.

62. Brichto, "Hebrew Bible," 217-19.

63. R. B. Hays, *The Moral Vision of the New Testament* (Edinburgh: T & T Clark, 1996), 295.

64. Cf. Forrester, "Political Justice," 1-13.

65. On this, see the critique by J. Boston, "Christianity in the Public Square: The Churches and Social Justice," in J. Boston and A. Cameron (eds.), *Voices for Justice: Church, Law and State In New Zealand* (Palmerston North, New Zealand: Dunmore Press, 1994), 11-35.

66. See, for example, C. J. H.Wright, *An Eye for an Eye: The Place of Old Testament Ethics Today* (Downers Grove, Ill.: IVP, 1983), esp. 40-45, 162; cf. Hays, *Moral Vision,* 208-9, 298-304.

67. R. Gascoigne, *The Public Forum and Christian Ethics,* 18.

68. Polish, "Judaism and Human Rights," 41.

69. For a brief survey, see H. D. McDonald, *The Christian View of Man* (London: Marshall Morgan & Scott, 1981), 32-41.

70. On this, see Cronin, *Rights and Christian Ethics,* 165ff.

71. The *Mekilta*—a rabbinic commentary on Exodus—suggests that the Ten Commandments were engraved on parallel tablets of stone, with each commandment being related to its opposite number. The first commandment, about the absolute sovereignty of God, is paralleled by the prohibition on murder. This arrangement, the rabbis teach, serves to show that to kill a person is to diminish the likeness of God, indeed to diminish the reality of God's self. As in Polish, "Judaism and Human Rights": 41.

72. For this insight, see Marshall, *Human Rights in Christian Perspective* (Toronto: Institute for Christian Studies, 1983), 20. On some implications of this for medical ethics, see M. Banner, "Christian Anthropology at the Beginning and End of Life," *Scottish Journal of Theology* 51/1 (1998): 22-6.

73. Montgomery notes that the biblical assertion that each person is their brother's keeper (Gen. 4:9-10; Luke 10:25-37) contradicts the common law doctrine of nonfeasance (i.e., a person is under no legal obligation to help a person in need and is not liable legally in tort of criminally for doing so, for example, ignoring cries of a drowning person), *Human Rights and Human Dignity,* 186.

74. C. J. H. Wright, *Human Rights: A Study in Biblical Themes* (Bramcote, Nottinghamshire: Grove Books, 1979), 10.

75. R. J. Clifford, *Creation Accounts in the Ancient Near East and in the Bible* (Washington, D.C.: Catholic Biblical Association, 1994), 143.

76. Moltmann also proposes that the common human identity of rulers and ruled alike implied in the creation story leads in principle to on-going historical process of democratizing the exercise of power through such things as a separation of powers, the limitation of the mandate to rule to a stipulated time, and an extensive participation in the political process, *On Human Dignity,* 23-26 (quote from p. 23).

77. Polish, "Judaism and Human Rights," 41.

78. Moltmann, *On Human Dignity,* 25.

79. See Marshall's helpful discussion in "Does the Creation Have Rights?": 43-47; also D. Jenkins, "Theological Inquiry Concerning Human Rights," *Ecumenical Review* 27/2 (1975): 100.

80. It is true of course that the rights implications drawn from the imago Dei are of a general nature and do not provide detailed guidance for running the political order or adjudicating between conflicting rights. To say each person reflects the divine image, Paul Marshall rightly notes, "cannot answer the *political* questions of how to deal with the interrelations of many people who are all imago Dei and who have possibly conflicting aims and purposes," in "Dooyeweerd's Empirical Rights The-

ory," in C. T. MacIntire (ed.), *The Legacy of Herman Dooyeweerd* (Lanham, Md.: University Press of America, 1985), 120.

81. Cronin, *Rights and Christian Ethics*, 181.

82. Cf. S. Greidanus, "Human Rights in Biblical Perspective," *Calvin Theological Review* 19/1 (1984): 6-13. Clifford notes that in the Genesis accounts, it is only after the flood that the real-life diversity of nations and cultures begins, *Creation Accounts*, 149.

83. M. Shupack, "Mexico and Human Rights in Biblical Proclamation," *MCC Peace Office Newsletter* 25/3 (1995): 11. So too Montgomery, *Human Rights*, 175-79.

84. J. Lochman, "Ideology or Theology of Human Rights? The Problematic Nature of the Concept of Human Rights Today," *Concilium* 124 (1979): 16-17.

85. Moltmann, *On Human Dignity*, 33.

86. Moltmann, *On Human Dignity*, 26; also Stackhouse, *Creeds, Society and Human Rights*, 5.

87. Admittedly it is problematic to speak meaningfully of God possessing rights (see Cronin, *Rights and Christian Ethics*, 243-50), but if God bestows rights, then in some sense they belong to God.

88. Ps. 8:5; cf. Gen. 31:1, 45:13; Exod. 16:7, 33:18; 1 Kings 8:11; Isa. 6:3, 10:3, 22:24.

89. For an exploration of this idea, see D. J. Bryant, "*Imago Dei*, Imagination, and Ecological Responsibility," *Theology Today* 57/1 (2000): 34-50.

90. Moltmann, *On Human Dignity*, 10.

91. Marshall, *Human Rights*, 20.

92. Moltmann, *On Human Dignity*, 27.

93. Wright, *An Eye for an Eye*, 24-25.

94. Wright, *An Eye for an Eye*, 69.

95. Kirk contradicts himself by first saying that rights exist in virtue of possessing the divine image (p. 11), then saying, "Rights are granted both because of and in spite of man's sin. In a world of perfect moral righteousness human rights are superfluous, but in a fallen world some human beings need protecting against the lust and violence of others," J. A. Kirk, "Human Rights: The Personal Debate," in J. Stott (ed.), *The Year 2000 AD* (London: Marshalls, 1983), 12.

96. On this, see Wright, *Human Rights*, 13-16.

97. The biblical picture of human beings being granted "dominion" over the earth is often criticized today for encouraging abusive and exploitative behavior towards the natural environment. But, as David Bryant points out, humans are inherently cultural beings with the power to shape and maintain their environment, so that possession of power in relation to nature cannot be avoided. Such power also inevitably involves an element of coercion to make aspects of the natural world bend to our wishes. The issue is not *whether* human beings have dominion, but *how* they exercize it, "*Imago Dei*, Imagination, and Ecological Responsibility," esp. 41-45.

98. Cronin, *Rights and Christian Ethics*, 258.

99. Cronin, *Rights and Christian Ethics*, 222.

100. For example, Sugden, "The Right to be Human," 47; Swaim, "Bible Proclamation," 4-5.

101. Barr, "Ancient Biblical Laws," 21ff.

102. For this, I am indebted to Cronin's helpful discussion in *Rights and Christian Ethics*, 183-232.

103. Brichto, "The Hebrew Bible," 218. Paul's judgment on this matter is that Israel did not succeed in her mission, but where Israel failed, Christ triumphed (see Rom. 2–3).

104. Israel could even understand God to bless her historic adversaries. "On that day Israel will be the third with Egypt and Assyria, a blessing in the midst of the earth, whom the LORD of hosts has blessed, saying, 'Blessed be Egypt my people, and Assyria the work of my hands, and Israel my heritage'" (Isa. 19:24-25). "Are you not like the Ethiopians to me, O people of Israel? says the LORD. Did I not bring Israel up from the land of Egypt, and the Philistines from Caphtor and the Arameans from Kir?" (Amos 9:7).

105. Brichto insists that "the fanatical biblical zeal for monolatrous or monotheistic worship of the Lord" was restricted to members of the covenant community alone.

> While the one true religion of Israel is seen as the model and exemplar for all peoples and nations, nowhere in the biblical record is there even the thought of exporting it in coercive fashion beyond Israel's territories or of subjecting non-Israelites to its canons of faith and praxis. In Deuteronomy the proscription of human sacrifice and nature-worship for the covenant community explicitly states that the Deity Himself has allotted such false worship to all the other peoples on earth (Deut. 18:9-14). While Israel's covenant with the one God is seen as a boon and privilege entailing the obligations of grateful loyalty, Scripture's attitude to pagan religion is one of condescension and contempt: the pagans are more to be pitied than loathed. Crucially, paganism is not in itself grounds for the discriminatory oppression of its practitioners—even within the borders of Israel's sacred territory. "Hebrew Bible," 226.

106. "The covenantal relationship between God and Israel is to be understood, then, as the same kind of relationship which the Deity would have between himself and mankind. The latter he holds in abeyance while testing Israel in that relationship. Covenantal law and morality, which applies to all members of the covenant community, is therefore prototypical of the law and morality which would apply to all mankind—were all mankind to constitute itself, as God has first willed, a covenant community. Every right enjoyed by an Israelite is thus, in ideal terms, a human right." Brichto, "Hebrew Bible," 218.

107. In this connection, J. Barr points to Psalms 1, 19, and 119 which celebrate the Torah. These psalms refer to commandments, statutes and ordinances without giving specific content and detail to them. Conventionally this has been associated with the Mosaic Torah. But some sug-

gest that the Torah venerated here is more like the vaguer and wider notion of "instruction" in the Wisdom literature—including an emphasis on God's wisdom being known in the created order—and being as universal as the sun and moon, like "natural law," "Ancient Biblical Laws," 28-33.

108. The term *mishpat* has a wide range of applications. It can refer to any of the practical components of litigation, such as arraignment, indictment, trial, verdict, sentence, penalty, as well as to abstract justice, to a law, to a series of legal decisions, and to norms or mores which are customary or conventional. Only rarely does it have the sense of pre-existing rights.

109. Barr, "Ancient Biblical Laws," 25-26 (quote from p. 25).

110. For a discussion of biblical teaching on righteousness and justice, see C. D. Marshall, *Beyond Retribution: A New Testament Vision for Justice, Crime and Punishment* (Grand Rapids, Mich.: Wm. B. Eerdmans, 2001), esp. 35-69.

111. See the major treatment of this by M. Weinfeld, *Social Justice in Ancient Israel and in the Ancient Near East* (Minneapolis: Fortress Press, 1995). On the wider vocabulary of justice, see Wright, *An Eye for An Eye*, 133-47; R. P. Knierim, *The Task of Old Testament Theology* (Grand Rapids, Mich.: Wm. B. Eerdmans, 1995), 86-122.

112. Henkin, "Judaism and Human Rights": 438.

113. Wright, *An Eye for an Eye*, 14; similarly W. Harrelson, *The Ten Commandments and Human Rights* (Philadelphia: Fortress Press, 1980), 13, 192-93.

114. Cassin, "Ten Commandments," 25.

115. For this way of connecting the Decalogue to human rights, see Wright, *An Eye for Eye*, 140-43; idem, *Human Rights*, 17.

116. Wright, *Human Rights*, 18.

117. Throughout Old Testament law, there is a tension between individual accountability and corporate responsibility. The individual is answerable for his or her own crime, but society must share the blame and experience the consequences (cf. Exod. 20:5; Num. 14:18; Deut. 5:9; Jer. 31:29). Corporate responsibility is shown especially by the way that Yahweh's judgment can be directed at the whole community in response to the sins of individuals. For a discussion on the contemporary relevance of this notion of dual responsibility, see J. A. Hoyles, *Punishment in the Bible* (London: Epworth, 1986), 97-109.

118. For details, see Marshall, *Beyond Retribution*, 207-8

119. Wright, *Eye for Eye*, 165.

120. G. Wenham observes that, "The degrading brutality of many punishments under Assyrian law is in marked contrast to the Hebrew outlook," in "Law and the Legal System in the Old Testament," in B. N. Kaye and G. J. Wenham (eds.), *Law, Morality and the Bible: A Symposium* (Leicester, England: IVP, 1978), 41.

121. Wright, *An Eye for Eye*, 165-66.

122. Knight, "The Ethics of Human Life," 81.

123. For a perceptive discussion on this, see Harrelson, *The Ten Commandments*, 107-33.

124. See Marshall, *Beyond Retribution*, 204-07.

125. M. Greenberg, "Crimes and Punishments," *IDB* vol. 1, 734.

126. Knight, "The Ethics of Human Life," 86.

127. R.Bauckham, "Egalitarianism and Hierarchy in the Biblical Traditions," in A. N. S. Lane (ed.), *Interpreting the Bible* (Leicester, England: Apollos, 1997), 263.

128. Evidence suggests that in pre-monarchical Israel an essential equality prevailed in Israelite life. There was little social differentiation in society; land was vested in the family, the clan and the tribe (rather than in wealthy individuals), and adequate provision was made for the landless. Things changed with the advent of the monarchy. There was increased accommodation to Canaanite models of social organization and conceptions of God, while the institution of the monarchy itself brought the reality of crown lands and increasing neglect of the disadvantaged sections of society.

129. Henkin, "Judaism and Human Rights": 438-39.

130. Henkin, "Judaism and Human Rights" : 438.

131. Cf. Knight, "The Ethics of Human Life," 86-87.

132. Polish, "Judaism and Human Rights," 47.

133. L. Epsztein notes that Israel was the only nation in the ancient Near East which did not take slavery for granted, which expressed sympathy toward the plight of slaves and which questioned, in certain respects, the legitimacy of slavery, *Social Justice in the Ancient Near East and the People of the Bible* (London: SCM, 1986), 119, 123-24. See also C. Osiek, "Slavery in the Second Testament World," *Biblical Theology Bulletin* 22/4 (1992): 174-75.

134. B. M. Ahern, "Biblical Doctrine on the Rights and Duties of Man," *Gregorianum* 65/2-3 (1984): 307; cf. Brichto, "The Hebrew Bible," 223.

135. See A. Schenker, "The Biblical Legislation on the Release of Slaves: The Road from Exodus to Leviticus," *JSOT* 78 (1998): 23-41.

136. See further K. C. Hanson, "Slavery," *International Standard Bible Encyclopedia*, vol. 4, 541-42.

137. See R. Bauckham, *The Bible in Politics* (Louisville: Westminster John Knox, 1989), 108-09.

138. Bauckham, *The Bible in Politics*, 103. See also W. M. Swartley, *Slavery, Sabbath, War and Women: Case Issues in Biblical Interpretation* (Scottdale, Pa.: Herald Press, 1983), 31-64.

139. Stackhouse, *Creeds, Society and Human Rights*, 273; cf. Brichto, "Hebrew Bible," 221-224.

140. See also Prov. 14:21; 21:13; 22:9, 22–23; 23:10-11; 29:7, 14; 31:9, 31:20; Ps. 11:7, 101:1; etc. For this theme, see Epsztein, *Social Justice*, 113-118.

141. When the biblical writers speak of how God has established justice and righteousness in Israel (e.g., Ps. 99:4, 78:5, 103:6-8 [cf. Exod. 33:13]; Deut. 33; Ps. 50:2 [cf. Deut. 33:2]; Ps. 119:142, 144; Isa. 51:7), they often have in mind the giving of laws to Israel at Sinai, which included social legislation for the nullification of debt, the release of slaves, and the freeing of the oppressed. See Weinfield, *Social Justice in Ancient Israel*, 183-95.

142. Cf. Exod. 22–23; Deut. 14:28-29, 15:7ff, 26:12-15, 24:14-15; Lev. 15:33-34, 19:9-10, 25:35-38.

143. Israel's intransigent oppostion to charging interest contrasts vividly with the practice of her neighbors and was intended to protect the poor from loss of land and slavery, Epsztein, *Social Justice*, 124-28.

144. For some such difficulties, see N. K. Gottwald, "The Biblical Jubilee: In Whose Interests?," in H. Ucko (ed.), *The Jubilee Challenge: Utopia or Possibility? Jewish and Christian Insights* (Geneva: WCC Publications, 1997), 33-40.

145. Weinfield insists however that the Jubilee institution had a real historical foundation in tribal Israel and was observed up until the time of the monarchy, *Social Justice in Ancient Israel*, 152-78.

146. See the several essays on this in H. Ucko (ed.), *The Jubilee Challenge*.

147. For the way Sabbath and Jubilee provisions applied to different ethnic groups, see R. Jospe, "Sabbath, Sabbatical and Jubilee: Jewish Ethical Perspectives," in Ucko, *Jubilee Challenge*, 87-91

148. H. Ucko, "The Jubilee as a Challenge," in Ucko, *Jubilee Challenge*, 1-14 (quotes from 2, 5).

149. Deut. 17:18-20; 2 Sam. 8:15; 1 Kings 10:9; Jer. 22:3, 15; 23:5, 33:15; Ezek. 45:9; Isa. 42:1ff; Ps. 31:4-5, 72:1. See further Weinfield, *Social Justice in Ancient Israel*, 45-56.

150. B. V. Malchow, *Social Justice in the Hebrew Bible* (Collegeville, Minn.: Michael Glazier, 1996), 31-49 (quote from p. 43).

151. J. R. Donahue, "Biblical Perspectives on Justice," in J. C. Haughey (ed.), *The Faith That Does Justice* (New York: Paulist Press, 1977), 108.

152. The notion of the solidarity of the individual with the community is pervasive in the Bible. On the one hand, the individual is summed up, as it were, in the community. The Israelite is summoned to participate in all forms of social life in and through the community. God's saving acts are on behalf of the community, from which the individual derives benefit. The community, indeed, takes on its own individual identity as the son of God (Hos. 11:1; cf. Isa. 43:6; Jer. 3:20, 31:9; Mal. 1:6, 3:17). On the other hand, the whole community can be represented by the individual. The king somehow embodied the nation. The sin of an individual could bring guilt on the community as a whole (Josh. 7:24-26, cf. 2 Sam. 14:7; 21:1-14; 2 Kings 9:26). And never was the importance and value of individual personality entirely eclipsed.

153. Knight, "Ethics of Human Life," 65.

154. Quoted in Montgomery, *Human Rights*, 215.

155. If humankind was created in God's image, and Christ is the image of God, it follows that human beings were created in the image of Christ, whose image Christians are now being restored to. See McDonald, *The Christian View of Man*, 39-45.

156. Quoted in Montgomery, *Human Rights*, 215.

157. Hays, *Moral Vision of the New Testament*, 100-101. So also F. J. Matera, *New Testament Ethics: The Legacies of Paul and Jesus* (Louisville: West-

minster John Knox, 1996), 48; K. P. Snodgrass, "Matthew's Understanding of the Law," *Interpretation* 46/4 (1992): 369-78.

158. W. R. Herzog III, *Jesus, Justice, and the Reign of God: A Ministry of Liberation* (Louisville: Westminster John Knox, 2000), 174.

159. D. Daube, *The New Testament and Rabbinic Judaism* (London: The Atholone Press, 1956), 257, 259-65.

160. On this episode, see Marshall, *Beyond Retribution*, 230-34.

161. For a detailed argument, see Marshall, *Beyond Retribution*, 77-92, 214-241.

162. On this, see Weinfield, *Social Justice*, 57-74.

163. For details, see Marshall, *Kingdom Come: The Kingdom of God in the Teaching of Jesus*, rev. ed. (Auckland, New Zealand: Impetus Publications, 1993), 76-93; Sugden, "The Right to be Human," 53-60.

164. On Jesus' "show trial" in Jerusalem, see Herzog, *Jesus, Justice and the Reign of God*, 218-46.

165. Herzog, *Jesus, Justice and the Reign of God*, quotes from 250, 251.

166. "Freedom of religion, in the concrete social sense of the right to organize groups on a voluntary basis around ultimate concerns for the sake of all, is the primary social factor is the historical actualization of human rights," Stackhouse, *Creeds, Society and Human Rights*, 275; cf. 34-39.

167. I borrow this term from J. C. Beker, "Recasting Pauline Theology: The Coherence-Contingency Scheme as Interpretive Model," in J. M. Bassler (ed.), *Pauline Theology* (Minneapolis: Fortress Press, 1991), vol. 1, 21.

168. 1 Cor. 11:2-16; cf. 14:34-35; Eph. 5:21-6:9; Col. 3:18–4:1; Tit. 2:1-10. 3:1-8; 1 Tim. 2:8-15, 5:1-8, 6:1-3; 1 Pet. 2:11–3:7.

169. E. W. Saunders, "The Bible and Human Rights," *Church and Society* 69/2 (1978): 51-52.

170. Bauckham identifies two different ways in which the egalitarian ideal of the biblical tradition expresses itself: by direct opposition to hierarchical relationships and structures, and by indirect subversion of hierarchical arrangements, where the structures themselves are accepted pragmatically but transformed from within to ensure they serve the best interests of all. The second strategy is seen most clearly in the household codes of Colossians (3:18-4:1), Ephesians (5:21-6:9) and 1 Peter (2:18-3:7), "Egalitarianism and Hierarchy," 259-73.

171. J. Stott, *Issues Facing Christians Today* (London: Marshalls, 1984), 149.

172. W. Stuntz, "When Rights Are Wrong," *Cutting Edge* 24 (June/July, 1996): 10.

173. Bauckham, *The Bible on Politics*, 111.

174. For evidence, see D. France, "Liberation in the New Testament," *Evangelical Quarterly* 58/1 (1986): 3-23.

175. For an excellent discussion of Paul's conception of freedom, see J. D. G. Dunn, *Christian Liberty: A New Testament Perspective* (Carlisle, England: Paternoster, 1993), 53-77.

176. On the singular nature of freedom, see A. O. Dyson, "Freedom in Christ and Contemporary Concepts of Freedom," *Studia Theologica* 39 (1985): 55-72.

177. Cf. Cronin, *Rights and Christian Ethics*, 133-82.

178. B. Gerharddson, *The Ethos of the Bible* (London: Darton Longman & Todd, 1982), 68.

179. See Bauckham, *The Bible in Politics*, 113-116.

180. Paul's attitude to slavery is complex and controversial. For an exposure to the issues, see N. Elliott, *Liberating Paul: The Justice of God and the Politics of the Apostle* (Maryknoll, N.Y.: Orbis, 1994), 32-66; D. B. Martin, *Slavery as Salvation: The Metaphor of Slavery in Pauline Christianity* (New Haven and London: Yale University Press, 1990); J. M. G. Barclay, "Paul, Philemon and the Dilemma of Christian Slave-Ownership," *New Testament Studies* 37/2 (1991): 161-86; G. W. Dawes, "'But If You Can Gain Your Freedom' (1 Cor. 7:17-24)," *Catholic Biblical Quarterly* 52/4 (1990): 681-97; C. S. Keener, *Paul, Women and Wives: Marriage and Women's Ministry in the Letters of Paul* (Peabody, Mass.: Hendrickson, 1992), 184-224; M. Davies, "Work and Slavery in the New Testament: Impoverishments of Traditions," in J. W. Rogerson, M. Davies and M. D. Carroll (eds.), *The Bible in Ethics*, The Second Sheffield Colloquium (Sheffield: Sheffield Academic Press, 1995), 315-47; S. Biberstein, "Disrupting the Normal Reality of Slavery: A Feminist Reading of the Letter to Philemon," *Journal for the Study of the New Testament* 79 (2000), 105-116.

181. On the limits of Paul's freedom, see P. Richardson and P. W. Gooch, "Accommodation Ethics," *Tyndale Bulletin* 29 (1978), 89-142.

182. Shupack, "Demands of Dignity," 254.

183. Shupack, "The Churches and Human Rights," 132-33.

184. Marshall, "Justice and Rights," 149.

185. On the role of patience, see Cronin, *Rights and Christian Ethics*, 201-8.

186. See W. Moberly, "Political Well-being in Biblical Perspective," in *Studies in Christian Ethics* 3/1 (1990): 14-29.

187. Marshall, "Justice and Rights," 150.

188. J. I. G. Faust, "Anthropology: The Person and the Community," in I. Ellacuriía and J. Sobrino, *Mysterium Liberationis: The Fundamental Concepts of Liberation Theology* (Maryknoll, N.Y.: Orbis, 1993), 506.

189. Shupack, "The Churches and Human Rights," 136-37

190. See Cassin, "Ten Commandments," 14, 23-24.

191. D. M. Smolin, "Will International Human Rights be Used as a Tool of Cultural Genocide? The Interaction of Human Rights Norms, Religion, Culture and Gender," *Journal of Law and Religion* 12 (1996): 143-71 (quote from p. 171).

192. Shupack, "The Churches and Human Rights," 144.

193. Moltmann, *On Human Dignity*, 17.

194. G. A. Haugen, *Good News About Injustice: A Witness to Courage in a Hurting World* (Downers Grove, Ill.: IVP, 1999), 67.

195. Forrester, *Christian Justice and Public Policy*, 246-59 (quote from p. 249).

196. On Paul's emphasis on the Spirit, see G. D. Fee, *God's Empowering Presence: The Holy Spirit in the Letters of Paul* (Peabody, Mass.: Hendrickson 1994); see also C. D. Marshall, "'For Me to Live is Christ': Pauline

Spirituality as a Basis for Ministry," in D. A. Campbell (ed.), *The Call to Serve: Biblical and Theological Perspectives on Ministry* (Sheffield, England: Sheffield Academic Press, 1996), 96-116.

197. W. W. Rankin suggests that the "sojourner motif" in the Bible, which confers full political and economic rights on on those without natural kinship or citizenship rights, provides a model or paradigm for conferring rights on future unborn generations, such as a right to an unpolluted environment, "The Sojourner Motif of the Bible and Obligations to Future Generations," *Saint Luke's Journal of Theology* 24/1 (1980): 21-27.

198. For an account of Jesus' teaching on the kingdom of God, see Marshall, *Kingdom Come.*

199. W. S. Towner, "The Future of Nature," *Interpretation* 50/1 (1996): 33.

200. B. Almond notes that one of the advantages of rights talk is the way that it focuses on issues from the point of view of the victim or the oppressed rather than from the perspective of those wielding power, "Rights," in P. Singer (ed.), *A Companion To Ethics* (Oxford: Blackwell, 1991), 263-64.

201. For an excellent comparison between secular, liberal conceptions of freedom as individual autonomy and the Christian notion of freedom-in-relationship, see Gascoigne, *The Public Forum and Christian Ethics*, 212-35 (quote from p. 213).

202. Shupack, "Churches and Human Rights," 136.

203. J. Rivers, "Beyond Rights," 3.

204. On this, see Cronin, *Rights and Christian Ethics*, 131-33.

205. Cronin sees one of the reasons for the bewildering proliferation of rights in modern times is the tendency to view all kinds of suffering and deprivation as harmful, without redeeming features and therefore the rightful object of claims for relief. But the belief that people have full control over their lives and automatic rights against pain and loss is illusory, *Rights and Christian Ethics*, 97-114.

206. For a full-scale defense of this view and an application to criminal justice concerns, see Marshall, *Beyond Retribution.*

Bibliography

Ahern, B. M. "Biblical Doctrine on the Rights and Duties of Man," *Gregorianum* 65/2-3 (1984): 301-317.

Almond, B. "Rights," in P. Singer (ed.), *A Companion To Ethics.* Oxford: Blackwell, 1991, 259-69.

An-Na'im, A. A., et al. (eds.). *Human Rights and Religious Values: An Uneasy Relationship?* Grand Rapids, Mich.: Wm. B. Eerdmans, 1995.

Banner, M."Christian Anthropology at the Beginning and End of Life," *Scottish Journal of Theology* 51/1 (1998): 22-60.

Barclay, J. M. G. "Paul, Philemon and the Dilemma of Christian Slave-Ownership," *New Testament Studies* 37/2 (1991): 161-86.

Barr, J. "Ancient Biblical Laws and Modern Human Rights," in D. A. Knight and P. J. Peters (eds.), *Justice and the Holy: Essays in Honor of Walter Harrelson.* Atlanta: Scholars Press, 1989, 21-33.

Bassler, J. M. (ed.). *Pauline Theology, Vol. 1: Thessalonians, Philippians, Galatians, Philemon.* Minneapolis: Fortress Press, 1991.

Bauckham, R. *The Bible in Politics: How to Read the Bible Politically.* Louisville: Westminster John Knox, 1989.

———. "Egalitarianism and Hierarchy in the Biblical Traditions," in A. N. S. Lane (ed.), *Interpreting the Bible.* Leicester, England: Apollos, 1997, 259-73.

Beaton, R. "Messiah and Justice: A Key to Matthew's use of Isaiah 42:1-4," *Journal for the Study of the New Testament* 75 (1999): 5-23.

Beker, J. C. "Recasting Pauline Theology: The Coherence-Contingency Scheme as Interpretive Model," in J. M. Bassler (ed.), *Pauline Theology, Vol. 1: Thessalonians, Philippians, Galatians, Philemon.* Minneapolis: Fortress Press, 1991, 15-24.

Biberstein, S. "Disrupting the Normal Reality of Slavery: A Feminist Reading of the Letter to Philemon," *Journal for the Study of the New Testament* 79 (2000), 105-116.

Blank, J. "The Justice of God as the Humanisation of Man: The Problem of Human Rights in the New Testament," *Concilium* 124 (1979), 27-38.

Bonino, J. M. "Whose Human Rights?," *International Review of Mission* 66/263 (1977): 220-224.

Boston, J. "Christianity in the Public Square: The Churches and Social Justice," in J. Boston and A. Cameron (eds.), *Voices for Justice: Church, Law and State In New Zealand.* Palmerston North, NZ: Dunmore Press, 1994, 11-35.

———. "Love, Justice and the State," in J. Boston and A. Cameron (eds.), *Voices for Justice: Church, Law and State In New Zealand.* (Palmerston North, New Zealand: Dunmore Press, 1994, 69-105.

Brichto, H. C. "The Hebrew Bible on Human Rights," in D. Sidorsky (ed.), *Essays on Human Rights: Contemporary Issues and Jewish Perspectives.* Philadelphia: The Jewish Publication Society of America, 1979, 215-233.

Bryant, D. J. "*Imago Dei,* Imagination, and Ecological Responsibility," *Theology Today* 57/1 (2000): 34-50.

Buckle, S. "Natural Law," in P. Singer (ed.), *A Companion To Ethics.* Oxford: Blackwell, 1991, 161-172.

Budziszewski, J. "The Illusion of Moral Neutrality," *First Things* (Aug/Sept, 1993): 32-37.

Byler, M. "Duties, Not Rights: The Glue of Social Harmony in China," *MCC Peace Office Newsletter* 25/3 (1995): 8-9.

Campesinos, "How Much Is a Man Worth? A Biblical Reflection on Human Rights," by a group of campesinos, *International Review of Mission* 66/264 (1977): 373-82.

Carr, B. "Biblical and Theological Basis for the Struggle for Human Rights," *Ecumenical Review* 27/2 (1975): 117-123.

Cassin, R. "From the Ten Commandments to the Rights of Man," in S. Shoham (ed.), *Of Law and Man: Essays in Honor of Haim H. Cohn.* New York: Sabra Books, 1971, 13-25.

Clayton, J. "Religions and Rights: Local values and Universal Declarations," in A. A. An-Na'im, et al. (eds.), *Human Rights and Religious Values: An Uneasy Relationship?* Grand Rapids, Mich.: Wm. B. Eerdmans, 1995, 259-266.

Clifford, R. J. *Creation Accounts in the Ancient Near East and in the Bible.* Washington, D.C.: Catholic Biblical Association, 1994.

Consultation Report: "The Meaning of Human Rights and the Problems They Pose," *Ecumenical Review* 27/2 (1975): 139-46.

Cronin, K. *Rights and Christian Ethics.* Cambridge: Cambridge University Press, 1992.

Daube, D. *The New Testament and Rabbinic Judaism.* London: The Atholone Press, 1956.

———. "The Rabbis and Philo on Human Rights," in D. Sidorsky (ed.), *Essays on Human Rights: Contemporary Issues and Jewish Perspectives.* Philadelphia: The Jewish Publication Society of America, 1979, 234-46.

Davies, M. "Work and Slavery in the New Testament: Impoverishments of Traditions," in J. W. Rogerson, M. Davies and M. D. Carroll (eds.), *The Bible in Ethics* The Second Sheffield Colloquium. Sheffield, England: Sheffield Academic Press, 1995, 315-47.

Dawes, G. W. "'But If You Can Gain Your Freedom' (1 Cor. 7:17-24)," *Catholic Biblical Quarterly* 52/4 (1990): 681-97.

De Gay Fortman, B. "Human Rights, Entitlement Systems and the Problem of Cultural Receptivity," in A. A. An-Na'im, et al. (eds.), *Human Rights and Religious Values: An Uneasy Relationship?* Grand Rapids, Mich.: Wm. B. Eerdmans, 1995, 62-77.

De Rosa, P. *Vicars of Christ: The Dark Side of the Papacy.* London: Corgi Books, 1988.

Donahue, J. R. "Biblical Perspectives on Justice," in J. C. Haughey (ed.), *The Faith That Does Justice: Examining the Christian Sources for Social Change.* New York: Paulist Press, 1977, 68-112.

Droogers, A. F. "Cultural Relativism and Universal Human Rights?," in A. A. An-Na'im, et al. (eds.), *Human Rights and Religious Values: An Uneasy Relationship?* Grand Rapids, Mich.: Wm. B. Eerdmans, 1995, 78-90.

Dumermuth, C. F. "Human Rights and Peace in the Light of the Old Testament,"*Theological Review* 8/2 (1987): 9-26.

Dunn, J. D. G. *Christian Liberty: A New Testament Perspective.* Carlisle, England: Paternoster, 1993.

Dyson, A. O. "Freedom in Christ and Contemporary Concepts of Freedom," *Studia Theologica* 39 (1985): 55-72.

Eastham, M. "A Critique of the Human Rights Tradition from the Writings of Gustavo Gutiérrez: 1974-1979," in B. Atkin and K. Evans (eds.), *Human Rights and the Common Good: Christian Perspectives.* Wellington, New Zealand: Victoria University Press, 1999, 77-96.

Elliott, N. *Liberating Paul: The Justice of God and the Politics of the Apostle.* Maryknoll, N.Y.: Orbis, 1994.

Epsztein, L. *Social Justice in the Ancient Near East and the People of the Bible.* London: SCM, 1986.

Falconer, A. D. "Human Dignity," in J. Macquarrie and J. Childress (eds.), *A New Dictionary of Christian Ethics.* London: SCM, 1986, 278-79.

Faust, J. I. González. "Anthropology: The Person and the Community," in I. Ellacuría and J. Sobrino, *Mysterium Liberationis: The Fundamental Concepts of Liberation Theology.* Maryknoll, N.Y.: Orbis, 1993, 497-521.

Fee, G. D. *God's Empowering Presence: The Holy Spirit in the Letters of Paul.* Peabody, Mass.: Hendrickson, 1994.

Feliks, Y. "Jewish Farmers and the Sabbatical Year," in H. Ucko (ed.), *The Jubilee Challenge: Utopia or Possibility? Jewish and Christian Insights.* Geneva: WCC Publications, 1997, 165-70.

Fletcher, D. B ."Human Rights," in R. K. Harrison (ed), *Enclyclopedia of Biblical and Christian Ethics.* Nashville: Thomas Nelson, 1987, 186-87.

Forrester, D. B. "Political Justice and Christian Theology," *Studies in Christian Ethics* 3/1 (1990): 1-13.

———. *Christian Justice and Public Policy.* Cambridge: Cambridge University Press, 1997.

France, D. "Liberation in the New Testament," *Evangelical Quarterly* 58/1 (1986): 3-23.

Gascoigne, R. *The Public Forum and Christian Ethics.* Cambridge: Cambridge University Press, 2001.

Gerhardsson, B. *The Ethos of the Bible.* London: Darton Longman & Todd, 1982.

Gill, R. *Moral Communities.* Exeter, England: University of Exeter Press, 1992.

———. *Moral Leadership in a Postmodern Age.* Edinburgh: T & T Clark, 1997.

Goldewijk, B. K. and de Gaay Fortman, B. *Where Needs Meet Rights: Economic, Social and Cultural Rights in a New Perspective.* Geneva: WCC Publications, 1999.

Gooch, P. and Richardson, P. W. "Accommodation Ethics," *Tyndale Bulletin* 29 (1978): 89-142.

Gort, J. D. "The Christian Ecumenical Reception of Human Rights,' in A. A. An-Na'im, et al. (eds.), *Human Rights and Religious Values: An Uneasy Relationship?* Grand Rapids, Mich.: Wm. B. Eerdmans, 1995, 203-228.

Gottwald, N. K. "The Biblical Jubilee: In Whose Interests?," in H. Ucko (ed.), *The Jubilee Challenge: Utopia or Possibility? Jewish and Christian Insights.* Geneva: WCC Publications, 1997, 33-40.

Greenberg, M. "Crimes and Punishments," *Interpreters Dictionary of the Bible,* vol. 1. Nashville: Abingdon, 1976, 733-44.

Greidanus, S. "Human Rights in Biblical Perspective," *Calvin Theological Review* 19/1 (1984): 5-31.

Hanson, K. C. and S. S. Bartchey. "Slavery," *The International Standard Bible Enclyclopedia,* vol. 4. Grand Rapids, Mich.: Wm. B. Eerdmans, 1988, 541-46.

Harakas, S. S. "Human Rights: An Eastern Orthodox Perspective," *Journal of Ecumenical Studies* 19/3 (1982): 13-24.

Harrelson, W. *The Ten Commandments and Human Rights.* Philadelphia: Fortress Press, 1980.

Harrill, J. A. "The Vice of Slave Dealers in Greco-Roman Society: The Use of a Topos in 1 Timothy 1:10), *Journal of Biblical Literature* 118/1 (1999): 92-122.

Hauerwas, S. "Why Time Cannot and Should Not Heal the Wounds of History But Time Has Been and Can Be Redeemed," *Scottish Journal of Theology* 53/1 (2000): 33-49.

Haugen, G. A. *Good News About Injustice: A Witness of Courage in a Hurting World.* Leicester, England, Downers Grove, Ill.: IVP, 1999.

Hays, R. B. *The Moral Vision of the New Testament.* Edinburgh: T & T Clark, 1996.

Henkin, L. "Judaism and Human Rights," *Judaism* 25/4 (1976): 435-446.

Herr-Zimmerman, B. and J. "Are Human Rights Universal?," *Mennonite Central Committee Peace Office Newsletter* 25/3 (1995): 1-3.

Herzog III, W. R. *Jesus, Justice, and the Reign of God: A Ministry of Liberation.* Louisville: Westminster John Knox, 2000.

Hoyles, J. A. *Punishment in the Bible.* London: Epworth, 1986.

Huber, W. "Human Rights—A Concept and its History," *Concilium* 124 (1979): 1-9.

———. "Human Rights," in K. Müller, et. al., *Dictionary of Mission. Theology, History, Perspectives.* Maryknoll, N.Y.: Orbis, 1997, 193-197.

Huebner, H. "Are Human Rights Universal? What Does the Question Mean?," *Mennonite Central Committee Peace Office Newsletter* 25/3 (1995): 15-16.

Jacques, G. *Beyond Impunity: An Ecumenical Approach to Truth, Justice and Reconciliation.* Geneva: WCC Publications, 2000.

Jenkins, D. "Theological Inquiry Concerning Human Rights," *Ecumenical Review* 27/2 (1975): 97-103.

Jessop, T. E. "Natural Rights," in J. Macquarrie, *A Dictionary of Christian Ethics.* London: SCM, 1967, 205.

Jospe, R. "Sabbath, Sabbatical and Jubilee: Jewish Ethical Perspectives," in H. Ucko (ed.), *The Jubilee Challenge: Utopia or Possibility? Jewish and Christian Insights.* Geneva: WCC Publications, 1997, 77-98.

Keener, C. S. *Paul, Women and Wives: Marriage and Women's Ministry in the Letters of Paul.* Peabody, Mass.: Hendrickson, 1992.

Kirk, J. A. "Human Rights: The Personal Debate," in J. Stott (ed.), *The Year 2000 AD.* London: Marshalls, 1983, 1-26.

Klenicki, L. "Jewish Understandings of Sabbatical Year and Jubilee," in H. Ucko (ed.), *The Jubilee Challenge: Utopia or Possibility? Jewish and Christian Insights.* Geneva: WCC Publications, 1997, 41-52.

Knierim, R. P. *The Task of Old Testament Theology: Substance, Method and Cases.* Grand Rapids, Mich.: Wm. B. Eerdmans, 1995.

Knight, D. A. "The Ethics of Human Life in the Hebrew Bible," in D. A. Knight and P. J. Peters (eds.), *Justice and the Holy: Essays in Honor of Walter Harrelson.* Atlanta: Scholars Press, 1989, 65-88.

Koontz, T. "Are Human Rights Universal?: A Response," *Mennonite Central Committee Peace Office Newsletter* 25/3 (1995): 3-5.

Langan, J. "Human Rights in Roman Catholicism," *Journal of Ecumenical Studies* 19/3 (1982), 25-39.

Limburg, J. "Human Rights in the Old Testament," *Concilium* 124 (1979), 20-26.

Little, D. "Human Rights," J. Macquarrie and J. Childress (eds.), *A New Dictionary of Christian Ethics.* London: SCM, 1986, 278-79.

———. "Natural Rights," in J. Macquarrie and J. Childress (eds.), *A New Dictionary of Christian Ethics.* London: SCM, 1986, 414-415.

Lochman, J. M. "Ideology or Theology of Human Rights? The Problematic Nature of the Concept of Human Rights Today," *Concilium* 124 (1979), 11-19.

Malchow, B. V. *Social Justice in the Hebrew Bible.* Collegeville, Minn.: Michael Glazier, 1996.

Marshall, C. D. *Kingdom Come: The Kingdom of God in the Teaching of Jesus.* Auckland, New Zealand: Impetus Publications, 1993, rev. ed.

———. "The Use of the Bible in Ethics: Scripture, Ethics, and the Social Justice Statement," in J. Boston and A. Cameron (eds.), *Voices for Justice: Church, Law and State In New Zealand.* Palmerston North, New Zealand: Dunmore Press, 1994, 107-146.

———. "'For Me to Live is Christ': Pauline Spirituality as a Basis for Ministry," in D. A. Campbell (ed.), *The Call to Serve: Biblical and Theological Perspectives on Ministry.* Sheffield, England: Sheffield Academic Press, 1996, 96-116.

———. "Paul and Jesus: Continuity or Discontinuity?," *Stimulus* 5/4 (1997): 32-42.

———. "Was Paul a Sexist? On Reading Paul in Context," *Reality* 4/24 (1997-98): 19-25.

———. "Paul and Christian Social Responsibility," *Anvil* 17/1 (2000): 7-18.

———. "'Made a Little Lower Than the Angels': Human Rights in the Biblical Tradition," in B. Atkin and K. Evans (eds.), *Human Rights and the Common Good: Christian Perspectives.* Wellington, New Zealand: Victoria University Press, 1999, 14-76.

———. *Beyond Retribution: A New Testament Vision for Justice, Crime and Punishment.* Grand Rapids, Mich.: Wm. B. Eerdmans, 2001.

Marshall, P. "'Cultural Context' Usually A Pretext for Repression," *World Perspectives,* April 12, 1994.

———. "Does the Creation Have Rights?" *Studies in Christian Ethics* 6/2 (1993): 31-49.

———. "Dooyeweerd's Empirical Rights Theory," in C. T. MacIntire (ed.), *The Legacy of Herman Dooyeweerd.* Lanham, Md.: University Press of America, 1985, 119-42.

———. "Innate Rights and Just Relations," *Koers* 56/2 (1991): 139-49.

———. "Justice and Rights: Ideology and Human Rights Theories," in S. Griffiden and J. Verhoegt (eds.), *Mirror and Context in the Social Sciences.* Lanham, Md.: University Press of America, 1990, 129-58.

———. "The Importance of Group Rights," in M. Charlton and P. Barker (eds.), *Contemporary Political Issues.* Toronto: Nelson Canada, 1994, 90-97.

———. "Two Types of Rights," *Canadian Journal of Political Science* 25/4 (1992): 661-76.

———. *Human Rights in Christian Perspective.* Toronto: Institute for Christian Studies, 1983.

Martin, D. B. *Slavery as Salvation: The Metaphor of Slavery in Pauline Christianity.* New Haven and London: Yale University Press, 1990.

Martínez, P. "The Right to be Human," *Evangelical Review of Theology* 10/3 (1986): 270-76.

Matera, F. J. *New Testament Ethics: The Legacies of Jesus and Paul.* Louisville: Westminster John Knox, 1996.

McDonald, H. D. *The Christian View of Man.* London: Marshall, Morgan & Scott, 1981.

McIntyre, C. T. "Natural Rights," in C. F. H. Henry, *Dictionary of Christian Ethics.* Grand Rapids, Mich.: Baker Books, 1973, 450-51.

Mendiola, M. R. "Human Rights—Content or Context of Mission?" *International Review of Mission* 66/263 (1977): 225-30.

Meyer, J. R. "Human Rights, Fact or Fiction? 'Human Rights and the 'Risk of Freedom,'" *Scottish Journal of Theology* 52/1 (1999): 49-81.

Milgrom, J. "Leviticus 25 and Some Postulates of the Jubilee," in H. Ucko (ed.), *The Jubilee Challenge: Utopia or Possibility? Jewish and Christian Insights.* Geneva: WCC Publications, 1997, 28-32.

Moberly, W. "Political Well-being in Biblical Perspective," in *Studies in Christian Ethics* 3/1 (1990): 14-29.

Moltmann, J. *On Human Dignity: Political Theology and Ethics.* Philadelphia: Fortress Press, 1984.

Montgomery, J. W. *Human Rights and Human Dignity.* Grand Rapids, Mich.: Zondervan, 1986.

Nash, R. H. "Rights," in C. F. H. Henry, *Dictionary of Christian Ethics.* Grand Rapids, Mich.: Baker Books, 1973, 589-91.

Nelson, J. R. "Human Rights in Creation and Redemption: A Protestant View," *Journal of Ecumenical Studies* 19/3 (1982): 1-12.

Nicole, J. "The Jubilee: Some Christian Understandings Throughout History," in H. Ucko (ed.), *The Jubilee Challenge: Utopia or Possibility? Jewish and Christian Insights.* Geneva: WCC Publications, 1997, 53-58.

Orlinsky, H. M. "The Forensic Character of the Hebrew Bible," in D. A. Knight and P. J. Peters (eds.), *Justice and the Holy: Essays in Honor of Walter Harrelson.* Atlanta: Scholars Press, 1989, 89-97.

Osiek, C. "Slavery in the Second Testament World," *Biblical Theology Bulletin* 22/49 (1992): 174-75.

Pagels, E. "The Roots and Origins of Human Rights," in R. B. McKay and H. Cleveland (eds.), *Human Dignity: The Internationalization of Human Rights.* Dobbs Ferry, N.Y.: Oceana Publishing, 1979, 1-8.

Pfürtner, S. H. P. "Human Rights in Christian Ethics," *Concilium* 124 (1979): 57-65.

Polish, D. F. "Judaism and Human Rights," *Journal of Ecumenical Studies* 19/3 (1982): 40-50.

Raiser, K. "Utopia and Responsibility," in H. Ucko (ed.), *The Jubilee Challenge: Utopia or Possibility? Jewish and Christian Insights.* Geneva: WCC Publications, 1997, 15-27.

Rankin, W. W. "The Sojourner Motif of the Bible and Obligations to Future Generations," *Saint Luke's Journal of Theology* 24/1 (1980): 21-27.

Renner, J. T. E., and V.C. Pfitzner. "Justice and Human Rights: Some Biblical Perspectives," *Lutheran Theological Journal* 24/1 (1990): 3-10.

Rivers, J. "Beyond Rights: The Morality of Rights language," *Cambridge Papers* 6/3 (1997): 1-4.

———. "The Virtue of Rights," *Studies in Christian Ethics* 13/2 (2000): 67-90.

Roy, M. *et.al.The Church and Human Rights: Pontifical Commission "Justitia et Pax" Working Paper 1.* Vatican City: Pontifical Commission, 1975.

Saunders, E. W., "The Bible and Human Rights," *Church and Society* 69 /2 (1978): 48-53.

Scharf, K. "The Human Rights of the Malefactor: On Visiting the Baader-Meinhof Group," *International Review of Mission* 66/263 (1977): 231-39.

Schenker, A. "The Biblical Legislation on the Release of Slaves: The Road from Exodus to Leviticus," *Journal for the Study of the Old Testament* 78 (1998): 23-41.

Shupack, M. "Mexico and Human Rights in Biblical Proclamation," *Mennonite Central Committee Peace Office Newsletter* 25/3 (1995): 10-11.

———. "The Churches and Human Rights: Catholic and Protestant Human Rights Views as Reflected in Church Statements," *Harvard Human Rights Journal* 6 (1993): 127-57.

———. "The Demands of Dignity *and* Community: An Ecumenical and Mennonite Account of Human Rights," *Conrad Grebel Review* (Fall 1996): 241-58.

Sidorsky, D. "Contemporary Reinterpretations of the Concept of Human Rights," in D. Sidorsky (ed.), *Essays on Human Rights: Contemporary Issues and Jewish Perspectives.* Philadelphia: The Jewish Publication Society of America, 1979, 88-109.

Smith, J. E. "Rights," in J. Macquarrie, *A New Dictionary of Christian Ethics.* London: SCM/Westminster, 1986, 556-557.

Smolin, D. M. "Will International Human Rights be Used as a Tool of Cultural Genocide? The Interaction of Human Rights Norms, Religion, Culture and Gender," *Journal of Law and Religion* 12 (1996): 143-71.

Smyth, G. "Sabbath and Jubilee," in H. Ucko (ed.), *The Jubilee Challenge: Utopia or Possibility? Jewish and Christian Insights.* Geneva: WCC Publications, 1997, 59-78.

Snodgrass, K. P. "Matthew's Understanding of the Law," *Interpretation* 46/4 (1992): 369-78.

Solomon, N. "Economics of the Jubilee," in H. Ucko (ed.), *The Jubilee Challenge: Utopia or Possibility? Jewish and Christian Insights.* Geneva: WCC Publications, 1997, 150-64.

Spray, P. "Five Areas for Jubilee Today," in H. Ucko (ed.), *The Jubilee Challenge: Utopia or Possibility? Jewish and Christian Insights.* Geneva: WCC Publications, 1997, 134-39.

Stackhouse, M. *Creeds, Society and Human Rights: A Study in Three Cultures.* Grand Rapids, Mich.: Wm. B. Eerdmans, 1984.

Stott, J. *Issues Facing Christians Today.* London: Marshalls, 1984.

Stuntz, W. "When Rights Are Wrong," *Cutting Edge* 24 (June/July, 1996): 5-10 (reprinted from *First Things*, April 1996).

Sugden, C. "The Right to be Human: Four Bible Studies," *Religion and Society* 19/2 (1982): 46-87.

Swaim, J. C. "Bible Proclamation of Human Rights," *International Journal of Religious Education* 44 (1968): 4-5.

Swartley, W. M. *Slavery, Sabbath, War and Women: Case Issues in Biblical Interpretation.* Scottdale, Pa.: Herald Press, 1983.

Towner, W. S. "The Future of Nature," *Interpretation* 50/1 (1996): 27-35.

Tanner, K. "Justification and Justice in a Theology of Grace," *Theology Today* 55 (1999): 510-23.

Turner, A. R. "The Human Rights Act 1993," in J. Catley (ed.), *The Vision New Zealand Congress 1997*. Auckland, New Zealand: Vision New Zealand, 1997, 365-84.

Tutu, D. "Religion and Human Rights," in H. Küng (ed.), *Yes to a Global Ethic*. London: SCM, 1996, 164-174.

Ucko, H. (ed.). *The Jubilee Challenge: Utopia or Possibility?* Geneva: WCC Publications, 1997.

Ucko, H. "The Jubilee as a Challenge," in H. Ucko (ed.), *The Jubilee Challenge: Utopia or Possibility? Jewish and Christian Insights*. Geneva: WCC Publications, 1997, 1-14.

van Egmond, A. "Calvinist Thought and Human Rights," in A. A. An-Na'im, et al. (eds.), *Human Rights and Religious Values: An Uneasy Relationship?* Grand Rapids, Mich.: Wm. B. Eerdmans, 1995, 192-202.

Vaney, N. "Human Rights and the Theological Tradition," in B. Atkin and K. Evans (eds.), *Human Rights and the Common Good: Christian Perspectives*. Wellington, New Zealand: Victoria University Press, 1999, 114-121.

Vasak, K. (ed.). *The International Dimensions of Human Rights*. Translated by Philip Alston. Westport, Conn.: Greenwood Press, 1982, 2 vols.

Vroom, H. M. "Religious Ways of Life and Human Rights," in A. A. An-Na'im, et al. (eds.), *Human Rights and Religious Values: An Uneasy Relationship?* Grand Rapids, Mich.: Wm. B. Eerdmans, 1995, 24-42.

Wake, J., et al. "Rights Stuff," *Issues in Ethics* 3/1 (1990): 1, 6.

Weinfeld, M. *Social Justice in Ancient Israel and in the Ancient Near East*. Minneapolis: Fortress Press, 1995.

Wenham, G. J. "Grace and Law in the Old Testament," in B. N. Kaye and G. J. Wenham (eds.), *Law, Morality and the Bible: A Symposium*. Leicester, England: IVP, 1978, 3-23.

———. "Law and the Legal System in the Old Testament," in B. N. Kaye and G. J. Wenham (eds.), *Law, Morality and the Bible: A Symposium*. Leicester, England: IVP, 1978, 24-52.

Westbrook, R. "Crimes and Punishments," *Anchor Dictory of the Bible*, vol. 5. New York: Doubleday, 1992, 546-56.

Weston, B. H. "Human Rights," *Encyclopedia Britannica* CD-Rom, 1996.

Wilfred, F. "The Language of Human Rights: An Ethical Esperanto?," in R.S. Sugirtharajah (ed.), *Frontiers in Asian Christian Theology: Emerging Trends*. Maryknoll, N.Y.: Orbis, 1994, 206-20.

Wingren, G. "Human Rights: A Theological Analysis," *Ecumenical Review* 27/2 (1975): 124-127.

Wright, C. J. H. *Human Rights: A Study in Biblical Themes*. Bramcote, Nottinghamshire, England: Grove Books, 1979.

———. *An Eye for an Eye: The Place of Old Testament Ethics Today*. Downers Grove, Ill.: IVP, 1983.

Subject Index

Scripture Index

158 Scripture Index

The Author

Cʜʀɪs MARSHALL WAS BORN IN Wellington, New Zealand. After completing degrees in anthropology and theology, he spent four years at King's College, University of London, where he completed a Ph.D. in New Testament in 1986 under the supervison of Professor G. N. Stanton.

During his time in England, he was involved in the leadership team of the London Mennonite Fellowship and since returning to New Zealand has retained close links with Mennonites in Britain, America, and Australia, including spending two periods of sabbatical leave at Mennonite seminaries. He lectures in New Testament at the Tyndale Graduate School of Theology in Auckland and has been widely used as a conference speaker in New Zealand, Australia, North America, South Africa and Southeast Asia.

In addition to articles on biblical and ethical themes, Marshall is author of *Faith as a Theme in Mark's Gospel* (Cambridge University Press, 1989), *Kingdom Come: The Kingdom of God in the Teaching of Jesus* (Impetus Publications, 1993), and *Beyond Retribution: A New Testament Vision for Justice, Crime and Punishment* (Eerdmans, 2001).

Chris Marshall is married to Margaret, a qualified lawyer who works as an adjudicator in the Disputes Tribunal, and has two sons, Peter (1985) and Andrew (1989). He lives in Auckland.